The Father's Intention

Making God Known Through His Sons and Daughters

By Phill Urena

To my Dad, Diego "Jack" Urena. Dad you may have been fatherless from birth, but you laid a good foundation in me. You were gone too soon, but you left a life-long deposit. I can only imagine the adventures we would have had together with my boys along the way.

Thankful for you and thankful we will be together again.

AND

To my mom, Carmen Urena. I don't think it would be possible for a son to have had a better mom. You always believed in me, believed I could do anything I set my mind to. From a very young age you laid a deep, deep, deep foundation of Hope, Faith and Love in my soul. So, thankful for your daily prayers, for my entire life. Love you mom!

Mom and Dad, together you demonstrated love and grace for the stranger, the orphan, the forgotten. You opened our home and took in strays and in so doing you formed in me the same heart. This book is dedicated to your memory, for all those that feel alone and misunderstood, to all the strays, orphans, marginalized and forgotten, who long for a safe place. I hope this book brings healing and transformation to their souls. I pray they would have a life changing revelation of our Father's love.

ENDORSEMENTS

Phillip Urena draws upon revelation from
Scripture, from experience with the Holy Spirit, as well as
the journey of a pastor who has served the church
faithfully for decades to create a beautiful portrait of the
power, purpose and plans of God's heart for us. *The
Father's Intention* assists in tearing down the lies and
misinformation we have all received about how God feels
about us and demonstrates through Scripture and
parables the truth of the depths of God's love for His
children. This book will change the way you think about
God, yourself and your reality.

Dr. Mike Hutchings, Director
Global School of Supernatural Ministry
Global Certification Programs
Global Awakening

Phill covers a lot of ground here: testimony,
theology, challenge, and practical instruction. Honest,
poignant, informative, and thought provoking, Phill's
book is a very worthwhile read. There are many
opportunities for the sincere believer to experience
transformative moments as insights into God's intentions
are offered, explained and applied. It will speak to your
heart the heart of your Father. I'm glad I read it.

David Harwood
Dirirector of the Love of God Project
Author of *God's True Love*

Some authors write out of knowledge, some authors write from experience. Still others will write in the third person. Phil Urena uses a compelling style of writing that gives you the feeling that you are on a journey with him. He combines his first-person illustrations with tested experience and a strong biblical foundation. When I came to the final chapter, I found myself in a new place in my identity and understanding of the love and acceptance of the Father. It's not just a book; it's an adventure.

Dr Ridge Burns
CEO, InFaith, Exton , PA

Let me be upfront about something. As of the writing of these words on January 1, 2018, I have never met Phill Urena. I have never met him, but I know him. I know him by his reputation as a pastor through many common mutual friends. Most of all, I know him because I know his son as one of our Nyack College alums. His son is a man of deep passion for God, integrity with his friends and commitment to the Mission of Jesus Christ. I saw in Jason the revelation of his father Phill. So while I have not yet met Phill, I know him. This is also the essence of this amazing book Phill has written. It is the intention of our Father in heaven to reveal His Glory through His sons and daughters. The revelation of the Father's heart drips from these pages written by His son Phill. Drink it in. You won't regret it.

Dr. Ron Walborn,
Dean, Alliance Theological Seminary

ACKNOWLEDGEMENTS

I would like to take a moment to acknowledge quite a few people who have been significant along the journey. I feel it would be remiss on my part not to honor them.

Don Sciortino, Lance Pittluck, Mike Turrigiano, and Randy Larson, I will forever be indebted for your mentorship in my early years of ministry, your friendship, and support at some of the hardest times in my life and your belief in me when I wasn't sure if I believed in myself. I still hear your words in my head and in my heart. Thank you!

To my brothers at arms: Rip Wahlberg, Ken Fish, Craig Simonian, Robby Dawkins, Steve Salsman, Bruce Latshaw, and Brian Blount - each of you have had a significant impact on me. Each of you encouraged me to believe I had something significant, timely, and relevant to be said. I am grateful for your friendship and support.

To my true brother in the Spirit for over 30 years, Dan Discoscia. I have no words to express how much your friendship means to me. More than anyone, you have encouraged me to write this book. Your belief in the importance of this material for this generation moved me forward.

Ann Jennerjahn, thank you for your friendship and the hours you spent reviewing my original writing, making suggestions, asking questions, and challenging me to say it better. You helped make this way better, sis.

To my daughter in law, Erinn, you challenge me to communicate well, and it has made me more intentional with my words. As I wrote this, especially in my time writing there in Redding, I often heard your voice saying, "Pops, is that how you want to say that?" Thanks for not being afraid to challenge me. You make a big difference in the quality of what I do.

To my sons, Jason and Matthew, what can I say? You are my joy as a father. You are my buds. It is amazing that, as a father, I can say my sons are also my dear friends. Doing life with you has taught me how to see my heavenly Father. You inspire me to be a better person and a more accurate reflection of our Father. The words in this book were formed in me because of you, your love for me, and my passionate desire to love you as He loves you. Every word here is a labor of love for my Father and for you. There has never been a man prouder of his sons. More than the stars, buds!

Now, the most significant person, my love and my best friend, my beautiful bride, Patti. You walked through the good, the bad, and the ugly of this journey at my side all the way. You are the perfect definition of "a devoted wife." This book is as much your story as it is mine. We discovered our Father's love as one flesh; I am so thankful for you. Who would have thought two fatherless twenty-somethings would walk through the adventure that has been our life and end up where we are? You are amazing, you keep it real and fun, there is absolutely no way this book would have happened without you. Thanks Babe, Forever!

Table of Contents

FOREWORD 1

INTRODUCTION 3

SECTION ONE: UNDERSTANDING A FATHER'S ROLE IN FORMING IDENTITY ...7

THE ROLE OF THE FATHER 9
A NAME ISN'T JUST A NAME 35

SECTION TWO: THE FALL AND ITS IMPACT ON MAN'S IDENTITY 47

UNDERSTANDING IDENTITY AND DESTINY 49
MISSING THE MARK 65

SECTION THREE: TWO FATHERS AND TWO KINGDOMS 83

THE FATHER OF LIES 85
OVERCOMING THE ORPHAN AND PAUPER SPIRITS 105
THE FATHER OF LOVE, LIGHT, AND LIFE 121
THE SPIRIT OF ADOPTION 129
THE FATHER'S LOVE REDEFINES US 147

SECTION FOUR: THE TWO KINGDOMS; THEIR CULTURE, ECONOMY, AND ATTRIBUTES 167

WHAT IS THE KINGDOM OF GOD? 169
THE POWER OF AGREEMENT 199

SECTION FIVE: THE FATHER'S INTENTION; SHIFTING OUR PARADIGM 209

THE FATHER'S INTENTION 211
SHIFTING YOUR VISION 227

SECTION SIX: THE PARABLE OF THE GREAT EAGLE AND THE VULTURE 243

FOREWORD

I met Phill Urena several years ago. A mutual friend told me, "Phil is a guy that is keeping all church leaders he is in relationship with pressing into 'the MORE of the Spirit.'" After speaking with him, I found that to be very true. As I have come to know him as a friend, I can say it's Phill's passion.

The Father's Intention is an invitation and a mandate. Phill invites us into a greater understanding of the war that we are born into. But it also carries us into the hope that the Father revealed through Jesus Christ to live in victory. His explanation in the section on two fathers and two kingdoms is worth the read alone. He doesn't just point to the destination on the map of identity and Kingdom, he invites us to join him on his journey of discovery.

The Father's Intention invites us into an encounter of the Father's heart, a profound depth of the Father's love, and an insight into the Father's plan for all to know Him through the demonstration of his Kingdom. I pray blessings on all who read this book! May all who do have eyes to see the wonderful, powerful, and liberating encounter awaiting you here in *The Father's Intention*.

Robby Dawkins
International best-selling author,
speaker, and TV personality
robbydawkins.com

INTRODUCTION

This book is the culmination of my journey of
discovering the Father, His great love, and the freedom
that comes when we fully understand the mission of
Jesus. Jesus came to make the Father known and destroy
the works and influence of the Father of Lies. Jesus came
to reveal the Father and bring the children home. When
He released the Holy Spirit, we were sealed into the
family of God with an unbreakable seal. If you believe as
I do, that God is intentional in every way to make Himself
known, to love and transform, to birth lovers of God and
people, then there is a message in and through your life
for His glory.

In Revelation 19:10, an angel tells John, *"Worship
God! For it is the Spirit of prophecy who bears testimony to
Jesus."* We may teach that prophecy is foretelling and
forth telling, however, in the heart of the gift is the
message of the goodness, kindness and love of God
revealed in and through Jesus Christ. The Spirit
communicates the testimony of Jesus to a dark world
searching for "true love." I believe an important part of
the testimony of Jesus is this: His Father in Heaven is a
good, good Father, and He loves us thoroughly. He so
loves man that He left nothing to chance. From before the
foundation of the world, He established grace and placed
it in the very fiber of the created universe in the person of

His Son, the second person of the Trinity. He did this, so grace would be all in all, so man would have all that is needed to come to Him, for His glory and man's great joy.

The beauty of the intimacy of God's love shared by the Apostle Paul in Ephesians 1 is amazing. True Love is not an emotion; Love is a person, the person of the Trinity. *God is love*, and He birthed us from Himself, leaving nothing to chance, establishing every expression of His grace in the very foundation of existence. This amazing kindness is perhaps the most powerful, beautiful, extravagant, and grace-filled expression of Love there has ever been or will ever be. It is still moving, forming, and transforming; it is an unstoppable force. He did this for you and me. This is not theology, it is a revelation of His passionate love and affection for His creation, particularly the masterpiece of His creation, His children. It is deeply relational, and it changes everything. It moves our theology out of our heads and roots it deep in our hearts, shifting our paradigm for this life, shifting it upward towards Heaven.

Lord, will you take every reader of this book into Your loving arms, and introduce them to Abba, Perfect Father. Use this book to bring wholeness to their soul and deeper communion with you until they come into the fullness of the Father's love. Empower them to carry this message forward in great love, the same message You proclaimed as the Father commissioned you, and to demonstrate your love with Signs and Wonders performed by Your Holy Spirit. Let us proclaim the year of deliverance, the day of vengeance of our God, and freedom for the sons and daughters. In Jesus' mighty name. Amen!

Section One

Understanding a Father's

Role in Forming Identity

Chapter 1
The Role of The Father

*Before I formed you in the womb I knew you, and **before you were born I consecrated you**; I appointed you a prophet to the nations. Jeremiah 1:5, ESV (emphasis mine)*

*See, I will send the prophet Elijah to you before that great and dreadful day of the Lord comes. He will **restore the hearts of the fathers to their children and the hearts of the children to their fathers**, and the hearts of the children to their parents; or else I will come and strike the land with total destruction. Malachi 4:5-6, NIV (emphasis mine)*

In November of 1981, before I was a believer, or at least before I knew I was a believer, I was meditating on the name of Jesus when suddenly the presence of peace filled the room and enveloped me. It was overwhelming. I felt like I was lifted off the ground though I knew I was not. Suddenly, I had a strong sense God was in the room introducing me to my not yet born child or children. I know this sounds strange. It felt strange to me at the time as well. I sensed a very sensitive, strong spirit. It felt like a poet's spirit; there was a soft-hearted love and a strength of character. I had a deep joy and sense of peace. I pondered at the time, *"What does this mean?"* All I could come to was for some reason, the Lord was touching me with an understanding of the hearts of both my sons, as they both carry something of this experience in them. They are both soft-hearted lovers of family and people. They both carry honor and grace. They are both men of character. Little did I know, six months later, I would need that experience to sustain my faith for six years. For you to understand why, I need to rewind to 14 months earlier.

On June 8, 1980, I married my best friend, Patricia Dougherty. She was stunningly beautiful, but on that day, she was more radiant than ever. She literally took my breath away as she appeared in the aisle at the back of St. Killian's Roman Catholic Church. I turned to my brother, Tony, and whispered, "Oh my God, she is beautiful." The ceremony and celebration afterwards were as near to perfect as a wedding day could be. Everything about those first few months of our marriage was amazing. We were in love, life was good, and the future was filled with hope. But after just three months of marriage, Patti became deathly ill. She had acute pelvic peritonitis. This was a terrible infection that, if not properly cared for, would cause horrible damage to her reproductive system, and possibly even death. To make matters worse, her doctor mistreated her. The proper care would have been hospitalization and IV antibiotics. Instead, he treated her at home. It took over two weeks to determine the right antibiotic and dosage. She was incredibly sick at home for a full month. I would rush home during my lunch break to check on her and make her lunch, while she lay in bed or on the sofa. She was in so much pain, unable to stand up straight. Our honeymoon season came to an abrupt crash. Finally, after a month or so, she could get around and soon returned to work. We didn't know at the time, but this would be just the beginning of her journey into despair.

For 18 months, we tried to get pregnant unsuccessfully. The same gynecologist who mistreated her decided to do a test to see if there was any scarring in her reproductive system. The test would inject dye and get images of her reproductive organs. After the test he said, "It all looks good. Just keep trying." He misled us, things were far from all good. At this point, we decided we would seek an infertility specialist and we found a terrific doctor. He was brilliant, kind, and caring. He was a teaching doctor at one of the finest medical schools in New York. We brought the film and test results from our previous doctor with us to our first appointment. After the initial examination, we met in the specialists' office. I asked him, "Based on the other doctor's images, what do you see?" He didn't want to say, but with some gentle prodding he answered, "Based on what I am seeing in these images, your wife is going to completely lose one fallopian tube, and at least one-third of the other." After months of further testing, surgery was scheduled. We were hopeful. After a couple of hours, the doctor came in to tell me what he had done. He said, "Mr. Urena, I am sorry to say things were worse than expected. The infection, almost three years later, was still present. It formed a cyst in one of the tubes. I couldn't save it. I was able to save a portion of the other tube, but I had to remove scarring from the ovaries, the bladder, and the surrounding area. I am sorry I don't have better news."

What did that mean? Could we or couldn't we have children? He sent us to a fertility specialist. The prognosis was not good, while it was not completely impossible, the likelihood was close to nil. There was almost no chance of having children naturally. He said we could try a few things but made no promises. With hope, we moved forward. We now had Jesus in our lives. We tried everything science had to offer and nothing worked. We were even among those included in the research of In Vitro Fertilization. Technically, Patti was even pregnant for about two months. A nurse came to give her injections daily. Again, we were hopeful... until she miscarried. Patti was heartbroken and hopeless. She was so sad and angry. For about a year after the surgery, it caused a strain on our marriage. We decided to move forward. She wanted to try adoption, but that door, too, was closed. We couldn't afford private adoption. Catholic Charities would not consider us because we were now Christians, not Catholics. Patti was heartsick. All she could do was "give it to God." Ironically, "Let go. Let God." was a wood carving on our family room wall. She did just that. One night in our house church, she gave it all to God. She wept and let it go; she surrendered. It was painful to see, but also beautiful as I watched her put her desire and passion to be a mom into His loving hands.

I was positive we were going to have at least one child. After all, I had that experience with the Holy Spirit all those years before. In September of 1986, six years after Patti became ill, my friend Drew Doxee invited us to a Vineyard Healing Seminar taught by his cousin, Lance Pittluck. Lance would become a big part of our early training in ministry and a dear friend, but on this weekend, he was just the teacher. After the last session, he invited everyone who needed healing to go to the back of the room, while those whose hands were getting hot to come forward for an impartation of healing. I went forward, and Patti went to the back. A man we never saw before or again ministered to Patti. He told her he felt she had some unforgiveness in her heart and helped her work through it. Suddenly, she felt heat in her abdomen. It was getting so hot it almost hurt, and then she felt a pop. At that point, we didn't really know what, if anything, happened. However, she felt lighter and experienced God's love for her in a new way. Approximately a year later, she was pregnant with our first child, a son, Jason. Jason means 'healing' or 'healing one.' God healed her and heard her cry to be a mother. Jason came two and a half weeks early on his mother's birthday. It was by far the best birthday present she would ever receive.

The best part is the story doesn't end there. Two and a half years later, in the early winter of 1990, while lying in bed one night, Patti said, "You know, I think the Lord said we are going to have another child." I chuckled and said, "He told me the same thing." Fourteen months later, our son Matthew was born, with personality to spare, funny, loving, and bright. Matthew, 'God's gracious gift' to us and others, was also born two and a half weeks early on April Fool's Day. I told the Lord, "I understand why Jason was born on his mother's birthday, your birthday present to her. But why was Matthew born on April Fool's Day?" His response was brilliant: "I love to confound the wisdom of the wise with the foolishness of God." You have to love His heart and humor.

He put the hope for our natural children in my heart nearly seven years before Jason was born. He hid in me a prophetic promise. He brought Patti gently to a place of surrender to Him. Then He gave us a double-portion blessing when science said we wouldn't have one. We were so thankful for one, but He gave us Matthew, so the world would know Jason was not a fluke. They both were given as gifts to us from our loving Father. He kept His promise to me. It is who He is. He doesn't just bless, He richly blesses those who place their trust in Him. That evening in November of 1981, before I understood how to be saved, God touched a man who deeply wanted to be a father with a hope that sustained him when man said, "very unlikely," and revealed the Father's heart to a man and woman for the first time.

The two verses at the beginning of this chapter are two of my favorite scriptures. I find great hope, peace, and confidence in them. They remind me of my Heavenly Father's hand on my life, and I am comforted by the reality that Jesus and the Holy Spirit are revealing to me this wonderful and matchless Father, who is perfect in love. Jeremiah 1:5 was my experience that autumn evening in 1981. Both my sons carry the gentle, loving heart, as well as a fierce sense of what is right. They both have the heart of a warrior poet, the same heart I experienced that night. They were in His heart and mind before the womb. In His kindness, Father God allowed me to experience the person and character they have, by His Holy Spirit, before I even committed my life to Him, knowing I would need faith in His promise to walk through that season with my wife. He is perfect in grace, kindness, and love beyond our understanding. He truly knows all our comings and goings and has prepared a place for us in Him. This experience released an ever-increasing faith and hope, empowering me to encourage Patti, with conviction, through that difficult season. A season that would start just four months after we were married and continue for seven years. He is good.

It gives me great comfort to know He also knew *me* well before He formed me in my mother's womb. Take a moment to contemplate this truth. He knew you before He formed you in your mother's womb. Say it out loud: "God, You knew *me* before the womb. You knew *me* and loved *me* before I drew a single breath." How is it even possible? For me, there is only one answer; I existed in the very heart and mind of God before the day of my conception. I was hidden in Him until the time of my "being formed in the womb." If it is true for me, it is also true for you. This amazing truth overwhelms me with humility and love. I was known before I was made. I was in His heart, waiting for the time of His release. From before a single thing was made, we were in Him. Wow! What a crazy thought. How can I be sure? Because God doesn't wing it. He knows the beginning and the end and everything in between. There are no details left out. "From before the womb, *I knew you.*" This speaks of intentionality and intimacy. He knew you before you were in your mother's womb! Intimately knowing every hair on your head, every desire of your heart, for good and for ill. He knew you and called you to be His. You were designed for His love. Crazy, right? Maybe, but it's the gospel truth.

It is amazing to see how Holy Spirit put the canon together with a central message about the Father. In Malachi 3:24, the very last verse of the Old Testament ends with a promise: *"The hearts of fathers will return to their children and the hearts of children to their fathers, and this will heal the land."* Some would say this prophetic word was fulfilled by John the Baptist. He preached repentance and a turning away. However, Israel did not receive it, and the Lord released judgment in 70 A.D. with the destruction of Jerusalem. I will not refute that claim. It very well may be true. However, there is something more here. Jesus came to restore the hearts of the children to Father God. At the end of this age, this truth will be more fully realized. When Jesus returns, there will be healing of the land. In the Garden, the planet suffered because we lost relationship with our Father. The planet is tied to the children. We were to take dominion over the planet, to be fruitful and multiply, to birth children who would love, worship, follow, and serve the living God. There is great turmoil in and on our planet as we approach that great day. The restoration of relationship to our Father has increased conflict over the planet. As birth pangs intensify, we see an increase in natural tumult, as well as conflicts of all kinds. As we approach the Lord's return, we will see an increase of these things, but I believe we will see many come to the Son and enter the Father's love. Throughout the Gospel of John, Jesus points to His Father. The Old Testament ends with this promise, and the New Testament ushers in the beginning of the process.

Many people would say Jesus came to pay for our sins and save us. Yes, He did come to die for us and offer us His life. I am personally so thankful for the Cross. Salvation came at the highest possible cost. However, the Cross is the threshold of something even more beautiful and more amazing. Jesus came to reveal the Father. He came to make the Father known. The joy set before Him was not our salvation alone, though He treasures our salvation and gave His life for us. No, this amazing joy was much more. It was the joy He had to see the Father's deep desire to have His children with Him. Jesus didn't simply die for us; He died for His Father's pleasure and purpose, so He could give the Father what the Father wanted—children who would carry His very presence in the perfection of His Beloved Son. He wanted His children back, and the Son was willing to do whatever it took to give them to Him, even at the cost of the most horrific death imaginable on the cross. The joy set before Jesus was not simply that we would be saved from the clutches of sin, but that we, His brothers and sisters, would be returned home to our Father's house.

The Enemy's Scheme

> *In your heart you said: "I will scale the heavens;*
> *Above the stars of God I will set up my throne;*
> *I will take my seat on the Mount of Assembly,*
> *on the heights of Zaphon. I will ascend above the tops of the*
> *clouds; **I will be like** the Most High!" Isaiah 14:13-14,*
> *NABRE (emphasis mine)*

Now, the enemy hates us. He hates that we get what he wanted, to be like God. We are not God, but we are His children made in His image, the image of the Living God. Through Christ and the indwelling Holy Spirit, we are being formed in His image to be like Him. My sons are not me, but they are like me in so many ways. We are going to be the "spitting image of our Father." Holy Spirit is working this process in us, "to the fullness of Christ." The devil is a liar, thief, and murderer. He tried to destroy our relationship with God, who *is* the source of life, and brought death into creation. Ever since, he has kept us captive as orphans, confusing us with lies that wrongly define who we are, and speaking into our souls an identity of shame, fear, and hopelessness. He's so good at his lies, he has shaped mankind into a dysfunctional, fatherless family, selfish and self-seeking, in search of an identity that will give us significance and self-worth, willing to take hold of it at any cost. This deeply rooted and overwhelmingly powerful fear and shame in our soul says we deserve punishment. This fear causes us to be profoundly proud. Pride is more than being self-centered; it makes us the center of our own world. Pride wants others to acknowledge our centrality and demands others meet our needs. At our worst, we see people as the means to our happiness, making us willing to do anything to survive. This is fleshed out in all sorts of ways, of which insecurity may be the most dominant. Out of insecurity, we are driven to illegitimate love and acceptance, purpose and significance, belonging and companionship, with little or no regard for others. We are powerless people, demanding other powerless people make us powerful. This ruins us and ruins others. I know this sounds harsh, but in our core, this is true. By the grace of God for most of us, this is not functioning in us at its darkest, but even just a little will destroy. Insecurity fleshes out our "me monster." It is all about me! Interestingly, we can feel like we are genuinely caring about others, while very subtly it is about us. Human love can be so insidious and self-seeking, yet so difficult for us to identify clearly. Let me be clear; I am not saying we are completely incapable of some measure of genuine love. I am simply saying, on our own, our very best falls far short of what true love is. The love described in 1 Corinthians 13 is a supernatural love. We only have access to this love by the Spirit of Love, Holy Spirit. Simply, however well we love, we are in a battle between self-seeking, human love and love that looks like God. Many years ago, I attended a conference on inner healing. The guest speakers were John and Paula Sanford, founders of Elijah House, an inner healing ministry that has helped many heal the wounds in their souls. While I don't remember much of what they taught, there was one thing John said that had a profound impact on me and has stayed with me over the 28 years of ministry since then. He defined human love as *"expectation, exploitation, demand, manipulation, and control."* Ouch! I am ashamed to say this has been the case in my own heart. It has also been the case in the hearts of many people I have counseled, ministered to, and pastored. As I contemplated this definition and worked through it in the laboratory of my own heart, personal relationships, and pastoral care, I found it to be true. We enter relationships, especially intimate friendships, with an unspoken expectation. Internally we ask, "Is this a person who might love me, help me feel more significant, or meet my need to be liked and loved?" In our search for a mate, we don't ask "Am I right for them? Will we be good for each other?" No, we more likely think, "Hey, they might make me happy." In friendship, we might look at the person as someone to fill a lonely place and be a friend in life, laughing, crying, and being a safe place. None of these things are bad. We were created for relationship. We need good, healthy, loving relationships that bring the best out of us. The problem is not the desire. The problem is often, we, unaware, are stepping into an exploitive relationship, most often mutually exploitive. When we have an expectation in a relationship we are exploiting, the other person must meet our own need. This is not love. If you don't know who you are, you will allow others to define you. You will do the same for them, leading to codependency. Codependency is highly toxic and destroys genuine intimacy. When we don't get it, when they do not live up to our expectations, we begin to demand our needs be met by subtle and sometimes not so subtle manipulation. Manipulation is an attempt to control, and control is likened to witchcraft. At its heart, witchcraft is manipulating and controlling someone for selfish purposes, for your own interests, or on behalf of another. This can never lead to life, health, or genuine love. Ultimately, this leads to toxic, codependent relationships, broken relationships, and broken hearts. In families, it can release a generational cycle of the same toxic behavior. In a dysfunctional role, this broken, self-centeredness of human love moves the leadership dynamics of a family into inappropriate roles that are not God-ordained. For instance, a family with an alcoholic or abusive father may force the eldest son to be the protector, taking on a role of surrogate husband to the mom, or father to the younger siblings. There is a rotation of roles in order to protect the family organism for survival. This can also happen in families with single moms, though many single moms do an amazing job amid incredibly difficult circumstances. My wife was raised by a single mom - her mom did the best she could. She is one of the strongest people I know. This isn't the only way human love creates toxicity and dysfunctional family dynamics. There are countless variables. Dysfunction is ultimately the byproduct of how sin perverts love into the selfish expression of *"expectation, exploitation, demand, manipulation, and control."* It is Satan's counterfeit.

In the Garden, we had a Father who perfectly loved us, gave us free will (the opposite of control), and loved us in true intimacy. When Satan usurped His place and the role of a father to define and impart identity, a counterfeit love was released, one that is all about self. We see this in the dialogue after the Fall. True love covers because His *"grace is sufficient" (2 Corinthians 12:9).* Human love is a counterfeit flowing from a foundation of fear and pride. Human love is not healthy love for self. Healthy self-love is humble, seeing and valuing our strengths as good and worthy of honor, while at the same time accepting our weaknesses, not as deficiencies, but as opportunities to make space for others to be honored and have a place. We do this not from a place of being less than another person. It comes from a place of humble confidence. We are satisfied to be who we are and to empower others to be the same, because we know we are unconditionally loved and accepted.

I am a visionary and a pretty good communicator. I see possibilities and know how to bring people together to apply their gifts, find fulfillment as a team sharing our talents, and watch everyone enjoy the result. I love to bring people together and encourage them in their gifts and calling. I love to coach the team and watch them enjoy the victory. But, I am terrible at maintenance. I want to always be building, improving, and inviting people into the adventure. However, I also want to see the fruit of my labor last beyond my life. I know that unless I mix my gifts with others who are good where I am weak, what I build won't reach its' full potential, nor will I have a lasting legacy. Unless I empower people gifted in ways I am not to ask questions such as, "What do we need to put in place to keep this going? "or "How can we do this better?", my results will not last. I need people who see things from angles I do not; this doesn't make me less, it empowers them to be more. It positions me to be both a blessing and to be blessed. It is part of Love and Godly Wisdom. I *need* pastoral-type people, because I am not naturally pastoral. The beauty of this is that once we see who we are, embracing our strengths and our deficiencies with confidence that we are significant even though incomplete, we start to see the gifts hidden in the people around us. We start to become His family. We make space and a place for others to partner with us in love and mission, with all the gifts working together as one, for His glory, the fame of His Name. This love helps and empowers us to be our best version of ourselves, the person God created us to be. Human love will always lead to counterfeit love and acceptance. Human love leaves us fearful of rejection and living in shame.

In the Garden, we lost our connection with our Father. God isn't simply a loving person; He is the very substance, essence, and presence of Love. For a believer, love is not an emotion; Love is a Person. Love is Jesus. Love is the Spirit. Love is the Father. The byproduct of man's rebellion was the creation of a void in our inner man. We had this huge love hole in our soul needing to be filled, so we fill it with those things that are incapable of giving us what we need, wounding each other in our vain attempts to get it.

The second part of this issue of love lost in the Garden has to do with identity. We were created to receive love, life, and light from God. These three are our intended source for all we need. Our identity is to be defined and realized through them. We are to be defined by love, life, and light, as they are the essence of the Trinity; Father, Son, and Holy Spirit. Love for the eternal soul is what feeds us and roots us in truth. Truth is light. It reveals what is real from all falsehood. It pierces darkness and keeps us rooted in God's reality. For us, Truth is a Person, the second Person of the Trinity, the Logos, Jesus Christ. As we rest in His love and light, we receive His life. In John 14:6, Jesus said, *"I am the way the truth and the life."* He was declaring that He, the Logos now in the flesh, was the Way — Love, the Truth — Light, and He is life, the source of all we need to sustain our body, soul, and spirit. The word 'truth' in the Greek is a fascinating word. It is *'aletheia'*, the unclosed, unconcealed reality. Jesus is saying to us *"I am"* your eternal reality upon which you build your life. Jesus is saying: "Let the reality of who I am define your reality." Allow this understanding to shift your perception of reality. Let Jesus be the paradigm you see all of life through.

Jesus came to reveal the Father, and in that revelation, everything else opens to us. Why would the maker of Heaven and earth choose to reveal Himself to us as Father? We can certainly say, "He made us, so it makes sense." However, this understanding falls short. One of the primary roles of a father is to communicate and impart identity. Identity is crucial in the growth of a child. Without a healthy self-view, we grow up to be an adult who struggles relationally, socially, and most likely, morally. Most of us are born into homes with some measure of dysfunction. Dysfunction can't communicate a healthy identity. The result is the vast majority of people have broken identities. The best we can hope for is something that resembles healthy relationship. At worst, we have the extremes of violence, rage, addictions, and abuse. A healthy identity is foundational to a life of blessing, fruitfulness, and love.

There has been considerable research in psychology over the last several decades regarding the identity crisis. As a Psych major in the early seventies, although I completed 18 credits in the area, I don't recall any meaningful discussions on the topic, not even in Child or Adolescent Psych, or even Abnormal Psychology. There is clear evidence today that the role of healthy fathers is critical to healthy child development. The research strongly suggests identity, false or true, is developed primarily through the father relationship.

"It seems to be that the issue of the decline of fatherhood and the problem of the male identity crisis are inextricably intertwined... So as we annually celebrate Father's Day, and reflect on its importance to social stability, more men in our culture need to find their male identity and commit to the central importance of fatherhood." (Ray Williams in psychologytoday.com, June 19, 2011)

In the same article, Ray Williams quotes David Popenoe, a professor of sociology at Rutgers University, as saying;

"This massive erosion of fatherhood contributes mightily to many of the major social problems of our time...Fatherless children have a risk factor of two to three times that of fathered children for a wide range of negative outcomes, including dropping out of high school, giving birth as a teenager and becoming a juvenile delinquent."

"One study of school age children found that children with good relationships with their fathers were less likely to experience depression, to exhibit disruptive behaviors, or to lie and were more likely to exhibit pro-social behavior. The same study found that boys with involved fathers had fewer school behavior problems and that girls had stronger self-esteem." (Mosley, J. & Thompson E. (1995), Fathering Behavior and Child Outcomes)

Identity communicates who we are, "our true self." One definition of identity is, *"the distinctive qualities of a thing that makes it unique from all others of its kind."* This means there is integrity between what something is said to be and what it is. It speaks of living and loving ourselves with the same identity God is speaking over us. Right identity positions us to walk in humility and love. It empowers us to honor others without being threatened by their gifts or talents. Wrong identity cripples us in insecurity and shame; it imprisons us in fear. We all have a self-view, our identity. Depending on who spoke it into us, we will either have a true and healthy identity, or an unhealthy and destructive one.

Let me share some of my personal story to highlight what is lost when we haven't had a father who can communicate a healthy self-view:

I was born in September of 1954 to a father who was literally a bastard; an illegitimate child who never knew his father. He came to the states from the Dominican Republic with his mother in 1923, at just five years old. His mother was a manipulative, controlling, and dark person. She was emotionally abusive and self-serving. They landed in Hell's Kitchen in New York City, a hard place known for its street crime and violence. He grew up in the streets as a fighter and survivor. At nine, he went to school and worked long hours shining shoes to support both himself and his mother, who had a parade of men come into their small apartment, sometimes for a few nights, and at least one for several years.

Needless to say, my dad grew up not knowing anything about what a father looked like or how to be one. He was a very hard worker, a person of honor and integrity, but he really didn't know how to father. He left home in the Summer of 1942, to report to boot camp as a drill instructor in preparation for the invasion of Europe, leaving behind a wife he had married just over a year before, with a seven-month-old daughter, Diana, and a son Diego (Jessie to the family) on the way. As far as I know, he hadn't seen his son, Jessie, but a few times as an infant. He spent nine months at the front, including the Battle of the Bulge. As part of the Timberwolves Division, his specialty was night fighting and infiltration behind enemy lines. He most assuredly suffered from PTSD, but at that time, there was no understanding of the condition. To add to the stress, my second oldest brother, Tony, was born ten months after he came home from Europe. He was cast into the role of husband, father, and provider, while coping with the pain and internal stressors common to the psychological aftermath of war. All of this combined with the expectation of transitioning into normalcy on his own, as if that was even possible. For my siblings, he was prone to impatient anger and for a season, disciplined them harshly, until my mom put an end to it. How was he going to communicate healthy identity to two boys and a sense of self-esteem to a little girl? He couldn't, though, to his credit, he tried.

When I came along, he was nine years removed from the horrors of war. He was beginning to adjust to something that somewhat resembled health. I was his second chance to get it right. However, he still didn't know how. Rather than rage, I received distance. He was there, but not present. He worked a lot, and when he wasn't, he was napping. Sunday was the only day that was his, and my mother guarded it for him. So, for me, my father was someone I looked up to and wanted to please, not so much by works, but by being a strong male, responsible, doing whatever was necessary. I did my chores without being told. I was there when he needed me to help. I wanted to serve him. To his credit, he was always appreciative, but not demonstrative in love. I innately had affection and empathy for him from a very, very young age and wanted him to know how much I loved him. I didn't know how to do that, so I became whatever I thought I had to be in the moment. It ended up forming in me what my dad called a chameleon personality. I could quite easily adapt to any circumstance or group of people by determining what I needed to be to belong. Hence, I was a chameleon, and I became a master at it. The obvious problem was I didn't know who I was, and there was no one there to help me navigate through a very lonely childhood and confusing adolescence. My brothers were terrible teasers. When I was little, they would tell me, "You were an orphan. No one wanted you. We found you in a garbage can in the ghetto. Mom felt sorry for you and made us take you in." They didn't realize or understand how painful and scary it was for a five or six-year-old to hear he was found in a garbage can in the ghetto. As teenagers they found it funny, but they were quite literally feeding lies that were reinforcing an orphan spirit in me. My mother would say it was untrue, but at my age, I didn't understand teasing. It hurt and made me question who I was and whether I was acceptable, or even if I was part of the family.

As I grew older and the chameleon took over, I found myself living in a subtle but crippling fear that there was no safe place for me. I had a terrible fear of abandonment and loss of loved ones. I thought if people really knew me, they wouldn't like me, and I would be completely rejected. Adding to that was the fact, I am a prophetic feeler. I sometimes feel the emotions of others. I was a dream and vision person from three years old. I remember going to a party in high school. I was very excited and looking forward to it. I was relatively popular and had no reason to fear rejection. When I walked into my friend's house, I suddenly felt rejected. It suffocated me to the point I had to get out of there. As a feeler, there were times like this when I felt other people's emotions. I didn't understand they weren't mine. I owned other's rejection as my own; I identified with it. I had been in ministry for years when I heard a teaching on the prophetic temperaments. The teacher explained that often the prophetic person wrestles with rejection. Their prophetic sensitivity amplifies the sense of rejection because they often feel other peoples' rejection and own it as their own. I would have short periods of depression and not know why. When I heard this teaching, it all made sense. Through those years, my saving grace was I had a passionate desire to know God. I always had an intimate conversational life with God, though I didn't have a saving relationship until I was 27.

Two weeks before my dad died, and just two months before my 20th birthday, he told me for the first and only time in my life he was proud of the man I was becoming. It was the closest I ever got to an "I love you, son." I am thankful to have had it. I cherish that memory close to my heart. It was the last time I saw my dad alive.

The lack of a strong father speaking truth into me and drawing out the good in me crippled me with a deep sense of loneliness. I was riddled with countless fears I masterfully kept hidden. On the outside, I projected a strong person—a confident and popular twenty-something who didn't care what anyone thought. The truth was, inside, I desperately wanted to be liked and loved. I was a tightly wrapped ball of emotions, with a terrible inferiority complex. I protected myself with an arrogance that said, 'This guy has it all together.' I was convinced I could never get 'it' right, and therefore, I would never be enough; inevitably, those I love will leave me. I will end up alone. All of this came together about six months after my father died, sending me into an identity crisis that ultimately led me to drugs and promiscuity to cope with the pain—not just of losing my dad, but of not knowing who I was or what it meant to be a man, with no one to walk me through the grief and confusion. The chameleon came out in full bloom, and I slipped into survival mode. I didn't grieve the devastating loss of my dad until my oldest son, Jason, was born 14 years later.

What a mess those first eight years after his death were. Three and a half years later, I fell in love with a wonderful, beautiful, amazing, but equally broken girl who had lost her father at three. She was also very much an orphan. We got married and started life together. Two broken young people, both fatherless, both survivors, both strong and stubborn, but very much in love. It wasn't easy, as we had to fight for every inch of our marriage. But the Lord was in it all, and by His grace, we made it through those first years until Jesus rescued us and started us on this journey to the Father.

We were made for the Father and the Son. We were made to live out of His goodness. My walk with Him has drawn me into Love. Not an emotion, but a person, the living God. Father, Son, and Holy Spirit. The process of discovering who I am was a process of surrendering my heart and life to Him. As He took my hand and walked me into freedom, I had to look at all the lies I had taken on as identity. It was a painful process towards freedom. Looking honestly at all the lies in my life helped me see all that was lost. I had to be willing to be vulnerable with the Lord, allowing Him to first show me the dirty garments I had clothed my soul in, trusting Him to take them off, and with them, my false identity. As He lovingly and tenderly walked me through this incredibly painful season that lasted nearly two decades, He began speaking to me my new, true identity: His sonship; you are a beloved son. It was worth it to get to the place of knowing and loving Him, and more importantly, knowing He loved me unconditionally. It is critical that good spiritual and natural fathers are raised up. I had no idea how desperately I needed and wanted to have a father. I also realized I could not be the father I so deeply desired to be without first knowing fully my Heavenly Father's love for me. We truly were made from love, through love, for love, and to love and be loved.

There is also a powerful and critical role for mothers, especially good spiritual moms. Please don't misunderstand me; moms are incredibly important and need to be honored and valued. However, we abandoned our Father in the Garden, and it has impacted how we mother and father. The world, in this hour, is desperate for fathers. My hope and prayer as you read further, is for your heart to be opened to the Father. Jesus came to reveal your Father and return you to Him. He said He would send the Comforter and Counselor who will lead you into all truth. That truth is found in the arms of the Father. May you have life-altering encounters with Love as you continue to read through these pages and be transformed by the Father who so thoroughly and completely loves you.

Chapter 2
A Name Isn't Just a Name

*The nations will see your vindication, and all kings your glory; you will be called by a **new name** that the mouth of the Lord will bestow. Isaiah 62:2, NIV (emphasis mine)*

*The one who is victorious I will make a pillar in the temple of my God. Never again will they leave it. I will write on them the **name** of my God and the **name** of the city of my God, the **new** Jerusalem, which is coming down out of heaven from my God; and I will also write on them my **new name**. Revelation 3:12, NIV (emphasis mine)*

I was born nine weeks early, in the very early hours of what would be a beautiful day, the 18th of September 1954. With the advancement of natal care today, it is not as scary as it was then. I spent my first few weeks in an incubator. I was a preemie, an incubator baby.

With the coming addition of another child, our home needed more rooms, and my dad was turning part of our attic into another room. My mom went to see the progress and fell through the ceiling. The floor had not been fully installed. She went into premature labor. As I was growing up, I was told she bled from the fall, and the doctors were concerned for both mother and child. My mom told me she was in pain and distress; she had already lost two children in pregnancy - one, my brother Tony's twin, and the other only a few years before me. She was frightened she would lose another, but when she looked in her hand, somehow, she was holding a penny. The words "In God We Trust" stuck out to her. She said an angel appeared to her and told her we would both be fine. She was told I was to be named Phillip Michael, after the evangelist and the Archangel, and that I would serve the Lord. I have very rarely shared this story for fear people might think it strange or that I was exalting myself. I can't speak to the truth of it or not; all I know is to my mother's dying day at 92 years of age, she held to this story.

Honestly, I never really liked the name Phillip. I would have preferred Michael. In my late teens, when I discovered the meaning of the two names, I *really* preferred not to be Phillip. Phillip means "lover of horses," and Michael means "Who is like God!" Many times, over the years, people have said to me, "Do you know what Phillip means?" I respond, "Yes, lover of horses. Ugh!" When I became a follower of Jesus, I wanted my name to be Michael even more. In fact, I seriously thought about using the name P. Michael Urena. As a young man, I thought it had a distinguished, even aristocratic, feel to it. The truth was, I just didn't like my name. I told a close, prophetic friend who teaches on dream interpretation the story of my name, and she said to me, "You are not getting the prophetic meaning of your name." I thought, "What prophetic meaning can 'lover of horses' have?'" She said, "Horses mean strength, endurance, tenacity. You have endured many difficulties, yet you have never wavered from your love for God and the proclamation *'Who is like Him!'*" For the first time, I realized my name was a prophetic declaration over my life. Maybe I could really believe my mom had an encounter with an angel who instructed her to name me Phillip Michael. I do not think it makes me special in any way. It simply means my Heavenly Father and beautiful Savior sent an angel to give me a name that would be a testimony of their goodness, kindness, and love throughout my life. It is a testimony of His love for all of us. While I was told this story about me, it is no less true for you. You're His child. You have a prophetic destiny. This is not about me. It is about Him and His love, and He has the same heart for you. Don't you know there is a day we will all get a new name? This name will be our eternal identity. What an amazing God He is!

When we look at the scripture, there are many stories pointing to the prophetic importance of names. They appear in both the Old and New Testaments. In Genesis 2, we find the story of Adam naming the animals. Often, we read over the story without realizing the significance of it. God created everything, and on day five, He creates the beasts of the air, ground, and water. God does not name them. He waits. On the sixth day, He creates man. He tells Adam to name all the animals. The story goes on to say there was not a suitable helper for Adam. This part of the narrative captures our attention.

We may tend to think the earlier part was just a prelude to set up the creation of woman. It is not. It is not like the Lord didn't know none would be suitable. He knew what He was doing. Do we really think God made everything, breathed into Adam, and suddenly realized He forgot something? No, both parts of the story have significance. Adam named the animals for two reasons. First, it was a demonstration of his dominion over them and responsibility to steward them with care. He was their lord. Second, it was to release a name that would be their identity. He was speaking identity into them. We also see this with the name Seth. Cain killed his brother, Abel. This had to be incredibly painful and confusing for Adam and Eve. It was the first murder and death they experienced. The ramification of their sin was right before them, as they looked at the dead body of their son, while they also lost relationship with the one still living. The fruit of the tree wasn't an illusion; it was now a reality staring them in the face. They had no understanding of death. No one had ever died, and most likely, they hadn't even considered murder. They experienced both murder and death in the heinous act of their first-born son and the loss of their second son. Adam and Eve are sick, confused, riddled with guilt, and grieving bitterly. They have no words to express the pain—a pain that never existed before this day. Abel is dead. Cain has been driven from them. A family is torn apart without any experience to help them process through these never-felt-before, incredibly painful emotions.

As time goes by, they are graced with another son to fill the hole in their heart the loss of Abel created. They name him Seth. Seth means *'put in place, fixed, appointed.'* This name is relevant in a few ways. First, Seth was not going to be lost. He was to be fixed, put in place of the one whom was lost, Abel. He was to stay put. This is significant. Notice, Abel is referred to as righteous Abel *(Matthew 23:35)*. The one who was righteous had to be replaced with one who is also righteous. Seth was the one who established the righteous line to Noah, Abraham, and David, and so on, all the way to Mary and Joseph's first-born son, Jesus the Christ. His name was more than a name.

A man by the name of Abram is called, along with his wife Sarai, to leave the land of his fathers and go to a promised place. I love the story of Abraham for many reasons. His obedience to go amazes me. Unlike today, when you left your family, you couldn't call them on the phone or skype, or take the car for a drive, or hop on a plane. No, when Abram left his family, he really left his family. Though he probably wasn't much further than the distance from New York City to Michigan, it took weeks of walking.

That takes boldness, obedience, and trust. In Genesis 17, the Lord visits Abram and changes his name from Abram to Abraham and his wife's name from Sarai to Sarah.

Abram fell facedown, and God said to him, "As for me, this is my covenant with you: **You will be the father of many** *nations.* No longer will you be called Abram; your name will be Abraham, *for **I have made you a father of many nations.** I will make you very fruitful; I will make nations of you, and kings will come from you. I will establish my covenant as an everlasting covenant between me and you and your descendants after you for the generations to come, to be your God and the God of your descendants after you...**As for Sarai your wife, you are no longer to call her Sarai; her name will be Sarah.** I will bless her and will surely give you a son by her. I will bless her so that she will be the mother of nations; kings of peoples will come from her." Genesis 17:3-7, 15-16, NIV (emphasis mine)*

There are a few noteworthy observations in these verses. The most amazing is their names are both changed by adding an "h". It is the same Hebrew letter that is in both the Hebrew *Yahweh* and English *Jehovah*. In Hebrew, this name would be spelled YHWH, as there are no vowels in Hebrew. The letter in Hebrew is like a breath sound. It is formed by releasing breath with a hard H, like a rushing wind sound. This letter is also in the word for Spirit in Hebrew, *Ruach*, which means breath or wind. There is little doubt that as the Lord calls Abram and Sarai into His purposes to birth a people that are His, He is symbolically adding this letter to both their names to express that their lives are now fully for His purposes. Their life is now in Him. He is putting His stamp on them and their progeny for generations, pointing to Jesus, *Yeshua*, (also an H) and perhaps even pointing to Pentecost when He will breathe His Spirit into their ethnic and spiritual descendants for the first time. The Lord makes a prophetic declaration releasing them into their destiny and changes their name just enough to mark them as His. Isn't it amazing? He wanted their names to prophetically point to Him and His purpose for their lives and their offspring for generation down through eternity. They weren't just names.

As we read further in Genesis 17, Abraham is instructed to name His son Isaac.

> *Abraham fell facedown; **he laughed** and said to himself, "Will a son be born to a man a hundred years old? Will Sarah bear a child at the age of ninety?" God said, "Yes, but your wife Sarah will bear you a son, and **you will call him Isaac**. I will establish my covenant with him as an everlasting covenant for his descendants after him." Genesis 17:17, 19, NIV (emphasis mine)*

The name Isaac literally means "*laughter.*" Whether it was a reference to Sarah's laughter or the joy Isaac would bring to Abraham and Sarah, who can truly know? Perhaps it was the joy the Lord would have by getting the last laugh. I have found the Lord has a good sense of humor. Perhaps all three are applicable. Isaac was a good and godly man. He had one wife his whole life, as opposed to both his father and his sons. He prospered greatly and lived a long, full life. His only pain would be not seeing his son Jacob ever again once he fled for his life from his brother Esau. Isaac is more than just a name.

We have a little different story with Esau and Jacob. In this story, Jacob is the younger of twin brothers. The name Jacob means "*usurper.*" This name speaks of how he grabbed Esau's heel at birth to hold him back from being first born, and ultimately how he cheated his brother of his birthright and his double-portion blessing. The story of Jacob is a particularly interesting one, filled with useful insights and practical lessons. Once Jacob usurps Esau's birthright, he must flee for his life to the land of his grandfather. There, he falls in love with Rachel and meets his uncle and future father-in-law, Laban. Laban is Jacob's equal in regard to scheming. Laban tricks Jacob into marrying Leah, after Jacob gives seven years of service to marry Rachel. Laban manipulates Jacob with another seven years of service, so he can finally marry Rachel, the woman he actually loved. Finally, Laban gives Jacob an opportunity to leave with a portion of his labor and go back to his home. Jacob ends up serving his uncle Laban for 21 years before he leaves. As he journeys back to the land of his father, he considers his brother Esau. He sends his family, servants, and all he owns ahead and spends the night alone.

*So Jacob was left alone, and a man wrestled with him till daybreak. When the man saw that he could not overpower him, he touched the socket of Jacob's hip so that his hip was wrenched as he wrestled with the man. Then the man said, "Let me go, for it is daybreak." But Jacob replied, "I will not let you go unless you bless me." **The man asked him, "What is your name?" "Jacob," he answered. Then the*** *man said, "Your name will no longer be Jacob, but Israel because you have struggled with God and with humans and have overcome." Jacob said, "Please tell me your name." But he replied, "Why do you ask my name?" Then he blessed him there. So Jacob called the place Peniel saying, "It is because I saw God face to face, and yet my life was spared." The sun rose above him as he passed Peniel and he was limping because of his hip. Genesis 32:24-31, NIV (emphasis mine)*

Jacob wrestles with what scholars would call a theophany: God manifesting in a physical form. In the wrestling match, Jacob dislocates his hip but will not let go. He knows this is not an ordinary person, and he insists on clinging to the struggle until he receives a blessing. The blessing he receives is a "new name." How could the one Jesus would descend from have a name with the meaning usurper? Jacob is no longer that man. No, he needed a name that would reflect not just his new life, but the nation he would become. He wrestled with man to find his way, and he wrestled with God to receive the blessing he so desperately wanted his whole life, a father's true blessing. His new name defined a people who would wrestle with man for their very existence, while not letting go of their promised blessing, just like their forefather. A name is not just a name.

According to some scholars, the name Samuel, or Shemuel means *"the one whom God heard."* This refers to Samuel's mother, Hannah, and her prayer for a child.

There are countless other stories we can share. There is John the Baptist, whose name was given by an angel to his father. John means "*Yahweh is gracious*" or "*God is gracious.*" Of course, John was the forerunner who preached "be baptized for forgiveness of your sins," and he pointed to the One who would release perfect grace once for all.

Jesus, *Yeshua*, means "*God is salvation.*" Certainly, a fitting name for the One who gave His life so we might be saved. The Apostle Paul was originally Saul of Tarsus. Saul means "*asked for.*" He receives an appropriate name change more suitable for his calling by the Lord. Paul means "*small one or humble.*" Could it be the Lord chose to change his name from Saul, the "*asked for,*" to Paul, the "humble," on the Damascus road to reveal his new calling? In the transition from Saul to Paul and his subsequent mission, the brilliant and talented student of Gamaliel became the humble bondservant of Christ. A name is not just a name.

We have a Father who is so amazingly intentional in love for every one of us. He has plans laid out for His children from before creation. He knows exactly what he made us for and how good it is. Our lives are significant and powerful, if we will believe. A name is not just a name; it should be a prophetic statement. The best part of the intentionality of our Father is He doesn't just have a plan for us this side of Heaven, but one for all eternity — an amazing plan we are each uniquely fitted for. We will each have a new name that will carry our true identity and our eternal destiny. His intentions for us are good, loving, and extravagantly beautiful. He has a name for each of us, and he draws us close to speak into our heart.

Section Two

The Fall and Its Impact

on Man's Identity

Chapter 3
Understanding Identity and Destiny

*"For I know the plans I have for you," declares the Lord,
"plans to prosper you and not to harm you, plans to give you
hope and a future." Jeremiah 29:11, NIV*

Knowing and believing your true identity as God's
son or daughter is foundational, not just for your life, but
for your Father's intentions. Your place in His family,
your gifts, calling, good works, and your purpose, both
now and in eternity, are intricately intertwined with all
God's children. He is working it all together for the
perfect fulfillment of His plans. Knowing and resting in
who we are positions us to unwrap the identities, gifts,
and callings of His children — our brothers and sisters. We
need each other to become all the Father intends for us to
be. How can you walk in the "good works" Paul speaks of
in Ephesians 2 without knowing who you are in His eyes?
Our "good works" are more than just fulfilling our
ministerial duty or life plan. You cannot separate God's
intention for your life from His love, or from His love for
others. All too often, we think of destiny as something we
need to do, a destination we must get to, as opposed to
something we become, and something we walk in daily,
as we walk with the Master. There are three parts to this:
intimate relationship with the Lord, loving relationships

with our brothers and sisters in Christ as we serve one another, call out the best in each other and honor other peoples' gifts and callings, and finally, loving and serving those around us, especially the poor and needy, both in the natural and in the soul. This is the calling of every believer. We are called to a life of love and honor.

As I write this book, I have been in ministry for just over 32 years. In those years, I have had the honor and pleasure of serving alongside countless saints who love Jesus. Unfortunately, all too often, they have evaluated their life on what they have accomplished in ministry. In the West, we like hard numbers to determine success. Churches should have growth; this is not a bad thing. The problem is when the things we can measure determine the value of our service and inevitably, the worth of our life. I certainly have been guilty of this, and it has caused me distress. Americans especially evaluate worth with measurable success. The weight of the system that causes us to measure success by numbers leaves many striving. If we don't meet the goals we have been determined as success, we are left with but one conclusion: failure. God does not see it the same way. I can't help but believe this flawed value system is part of the Fall. Not once in all my years of ministry has the Lord asked me, "How big is your church?" or "How are you going to grow it more?" Thankfully, this has not been the standard of His measure of me. If it were, I would be a miserable failure. What He has asked me is, "Are you loving people well? Are they growing more in love with Me and better at loving others because of your leadership? Are they learning to love themselves and walk in humility? Are they experiencing godly transformation?" Thankfully, I believe for the most part, I can say a resounding yes to all those questions. The motivation behind those questions is to be a better lover of God and people, something we will strive to improve upon as long as we are on this side of Heaven. Love, God-love, doesn't come naturally to this fallen race. We need Holy Spirit to help, and we need to be devoted to our growth. We need to surrender to love sacrificially. Loving like the Lord is sacrificial. True love is always sacrificial because its motivation is not towards self. It is the pursuit of selfless love that transforms lives. It is part of redemption's process. Paul speaks of this love in Ephesians 3:17-19, when he prays we would be rooted and founded in love TOGETHER with all the saints… "*to know the love of Christ which surpasses knowledge, that you may be filled up to all the fullness of God.*" As we love God and each other, we move towards being filled up to ALL the fullness of Christ. I don't even know what to do with that. We are going to be filled up with all that is in our beautiful Savior: the capacity to love, to release breakthrough, to experience the Father and the Spirit. I can't wait for the glorious day when we are filled to all the fullness of Christ.

If we have a healthy identity and are secure in who we are, we will have a successful life. Not simply in terms of the world's success, but relationally with God and others. Identity gives rise to powerful people who have the authority to speak into darkness and release His light, whether it is sitting across the table in a coffee shop with a lost soul, in line at the supermarket, talking to the neighbor next door, or in the workplace. We carry the Kingdom. We carry the King wherever we go. Jesus influenced not only the poor, but also powerful people. Amongst those He influenced were several rabbis, a Roman centurion, town officials, and the wealthy. We all too often miss that point.

We are His children, being filled to the *fullness of Christ*, conformed to the image of His Son.

> *For whom **He foreknew**, He also predestined to be conformed to the image of His Son, so He might be the firstborn among many brethren...Romans 8:29, NKJV (emphasis mine)*

This is a profound identity and destiny statement in so many ways, not the least of which the confirmation, we are His children, Christ being the "first born of many brothers and sisters." Given that we were created to walk in the identity of sonship, how did we lose ourselves? How did we lose our identity? That is where the serpent entered the story.

In the Garden, There Were Two Trees

> *Now the Lord God had planted a garden in the east, in Eden; and there he put the man he had formed. The Lord God made all kinds of trees grow out of the ground – trees that were pleasing to the eye and good for food. In the middle of the garden were the tree of life and the tree of the knowledge of good and evil. Genesis 2:8-9, NIV*

When I was young and heard the Creation story, I would sometimes question, *"Why would God put an evil tree in the Garden?"* I knew it said tree of the *knowledge* of good and evil, but my application was that it was the evil tree, while the Tree of Life was the good tree. The tree of the knowledge of good and evil was neither good nor bad in and of itself. It was a tree of relational choices. It was a tree of lost innocence. It was a tree of opportunity to be self-sufficient, to choose the God who is perfect love, or the darkness and depravity of full-blown rebellion. In the Garden, we had an opportunity to choose the Father, Son, and Spirit and receive life, love, and perfect light. Nowhere does the Bible say the tree of knowledge was evil. The choice to obey or disobey the command *"do not eat"* held the potential of evil. Immature, self-centered children test the boundaries of obedience, not fully understanding where disobedience leads. The immature do not make good decisions. Adam and Eve made the worst possible decision.

And all the inhabitants of the earth will fall down in adoration and pay him homage, everyone whose name has not been recorded in the Book of Life of the Lamb that was slain [in sacrifice] from the foundation of the world.
Revelation 13:8, (Amplified Bible)

I remember thinking, "I am so thankful God had a plan B—Jesus." The reality is, God never had a Plan B; it has always been Plan A. He was not stunned by what happened. He didn't step back, aghast, and say, "Uh oh, I didn't see that coming. What do we do now?" No, before creation, Christ was slain, and grace released (Ephesians 1:4-9 and Revelation 13:8). Nothing was left to chance; chance is not in His vocabulary. He always had and always will have it all covered. Isn't this great news? Let's spend a little time looking at the story.

This part of the story has Eve walking around the Garden and coming to a location in the middle of the Garden where the two trees were planted. Perhaps in her immaturity, she was already gazing upon the luscious fruit on the tree she could not eat. While it may seem like she was made yesterday, the truth is we have no idea how long they were in the Garden at this point in the story. It could have been eons by our measure. In any event, she clearly had no understanding of the risk, nor a full understanding of the Lord. However long she and Adam were there, they hadn't fully understood the Father's heart for them. It was impossible for them to understand evil in a personal way. It was so foreign to them. They only knew the Lord, Elohim.

So, here is Eve hanging by the tree she could not eat of. We would say, "Don't even go near it. Stay away." But she is there. She doesn't grasp the risk. Perhaps she was there looking at the two trees and contemplating why she could eat from one and not the other. All she knew was peace and love. Evil would have been just a word. Without the experience of evil, how could she understand it? Perhaps it was just such curiosity that allowed Satan to take advantage of the situation. He used the same tactics on Jesus in the wilderness, and he uses the same tactics on man today. Let's look at the conversation with Eve.

Now the serpent was more crafty than any of the wild animals the Lord God had made. He said to the woman, **"Did God really say, 'You must not eat from any tree in the garden'?"** *The woman said to the serpent,* **"We may eat fruit from the trees in the garden, but God did say, 'You must not eat fruit from the tree that is in the middle of the garden, and you must not touch it, or you will die.'"** **"You will not certainly die,"** *the serpent said to the woman.* **"For God knows that when you eat from it your eyes will be opened, and you will be like God, knowing good and evil."** *Genesis 3:1-4, NIV (emphasis mine)*

He starts by asking a question. It seems innocent enough. After all, she could have answered and walked away. The problem is once you enter a conversation with the devil, you empower him to speak into you. He is very good at speaking just enough truth to draw you closer, and the longer the conversation goes on, the more dangerous it becomes. Hence the reason James, in chapter four of his epistle, says, *"Submit yourselves, then, to God.* **Resist the devil, and he will flee** *from you."* A practical way for us to say this is, "Trust in God's heart for you, and say *no* to the devil's conversation." The question Satan asks Eve is very similar to the questions he asked Jesus in the wilderness, *"If you are the Son…"* Both conversations are strategically designed to raise doubt.

"Are you sure God is a good, faithful, and trustworthy Father? Did God say?" Satan asks Eve. Unlike Jesus, Eve does not speak a word of truth, but instead, makes a statement clarifying what God said, when all she needed to say was, "He said not to eat or touch it," and walk away. She explained it and began a conversation. She made herself open to the serpent's manipulations. I find it interesting that his reasoning to tempt her was to take that which she was already given and what Satan wanted: to be like God. We were made in God's image to be like Him. This does not mean we are Him—there is only one Eternal Father and Everlasting God—but we are His offspring. In Ephesians 3, Paul says, *"We are to be filled to the measure of all the fullness of God."* In 1 John 3:2, the beloved Apostle John says, *"Dear friends, now we are children of God, and what we will be has not yet been made known. But we know that when Christ appears, we shall **be like** him, for we shall see Him as He is."* The devil is masterfully devious at mixing truth with lies. He entices Eve with the very thing she was made for, "to be like God," and the thing he most coveted, *"to be like God and thereby steal the Lord's worship,"* Isaiah 14:14. At this point in the story, there is still hope for mankind, as Adam had not done anything wrong. Since the line comes from the Father, we still had hope.

Evidently, Adam is standing there watching and listening to the conversation. There is no indication he agreed until after Eve eats the fruit. Perhaps the sin of Adam was, in that moment, he desired his wife above God or he also bought the lie. Whatever the motive, he ate the fruit, and something dramatically changed. They both were clothed in "shame." For the first time, they saw they were naked. *The Lord God called for the man, 'Where are you?' He answered, 'I heard you in the garden, and I was afraid because I was naked; so, I hid.'* For the first time, Adam experienced fear and shame.

Fear and shame drive people into hiding. Guilt is an emotion that says, "I have done something wrong." Shame is an identity that says, "I am something wrong." Suddenly, due to the separation from God, we have the revelation, "I am not right anymore." What I was, I now am not, and what I am is not good. At this moment, an evil stepfather steps into our lives as an abuser, liar, and destroyer—a tyrant who hates us for what we represent. In his arrogance, the enemy thought he defeated God's plan; what he really did was set into motion the fullness of God's plan. Christ would come in the flesh, lay down his life, be lifted on high enthroned forever, release His Spirit, and raise up a family of Spirit-filled sons and daughters who will soon crush Satan under their feet (Romans 16:20).

Rabbi Dr. Hillel ben David of betnuma.org, in his study on "The Tree of The Knowledge of Good and Evil", shared a profound statement. He said, "The difference between before and after man's sin was the internalization of the evil inclination. Before eating of the tree, Eve had to be convinced by a snake, something outside of herself, to disobey God, and Adam in turn had to be convinced by Eve, neither would have sinned on their own." Before the fall, sin was unknown to man; it existed, but not in their experience. After the Fall, what was external became internalized in Adam and Eve. Sin is missing the mark of perfect love. Perfect love is the bullseye we are targeting. When we miss the mark, it is called sin. Sin existed before Eve ate the fruit. It existed in Satan and the fallen angels. It existed within creation, but outside of mankind's experience. It was now present in their very flesh and soul (emotions, will, thoughts, passions, and creativity). The self-indulgent passions were released into mankind's very being. The resulting effect was a new, false identity. They shed the identity of a son and daughter of God and received the identity of self-hate, shame, and all that goes with the orphan spirit. They go from peace and love to fear. They go from perfect acceptance to shame. Since the Garden, the enemy has been sowing false identities to steer us away from our God and Father, keeping us in bondage to lies that have stolen our sonship, destiny, and legacy, but most of all, our ability to receive and rest in God's love.

The Tree of Life

The Tree of Life was the provision of "grace" in the Garden. It was the means to sustain us in righteousness, truth and love. It was God's way of being our sustenance in a real and dynamic way. We could say the Tree of Life was a type of Christ, who would be nailed to a tree and become our "Bread of Life." The Tree appears to be more than a type; it was the means to real spiritual nourishment that would feed us in some real way, as we were told we could eat of it. As it was God's provision for us, it was obviously good. It was the means for us to grow in dependence on Him for all we need, as He now and forever will be the source of true life for us. It was both a natural source of life, *"you may eat of its fruit"* and a spiritual food. It was provision for eternal life, as we see in Genesis 3:22. The Lord sends them out of the Garden, *"lest they take and eat of the Tree of Life, and live forever."* It is important for us to understand we are spirit beings first. As our spirit goes, so goes our soul.

In the Greek, the word for life is *zoe*. This word refers to both physical and spiritual life. *Zoe* comes from and is sustained by the Self-Sustaining One, the Self Existent God.

> *"The Lord intimately shares His Gift of Life with people, creating each in His image which gives all the capacity to know His eternal life." (Strong's Concordance, word reference 2222)*

From the beginning, the Lord provided the source for spiritual and physical life through Him and Him alone. We now have access to this life through Christ. All others are a cheap and self-destructive counterfeit.

When I was first married, I worked in the rare coin business. The company I worked for was a large one, with several hundred employees. I became friendly with the buyers and graders in the company. I was a sales manager, and the owner and founder wanted us all to take a course in numismatics: the study of collectable and rare coins. The courses were taught at one of the local universities. Every Saturday morning for two semesters, I sat in a classroom or laboratory from 10 a.m. to 1 p.m. and learned about rare coins. One of the courses covered how to determine if a coin was the genuine item or a counterfeit. We looked at hundreds, if not thousands of gold and silver coins. They were all authentic coins and considered the highest quality — uncirculated. After a few weeks, we wondered if we would study counterfeit coins. After all, we were here to learn how to identify a counterfeit. All we had done up to that point was look at real ones under microscopes, noting in detail all the perfections, depths of the mint strike, and detail in the engravings. Finally, we asked, "When are we going to see some counterfeits?" The instructor's response has stuck with me to this day. "When you know every detail of the real thing, when you are so familiar with what an authentic coin in pristine condition looks like, the counterfeit will be obvious. If you are completely familiar with every detail of the authentic, a counterfeit will never slip by you." The same is true with the Lord. When we come to know His heart and mind well, no lie will be able to get past us. Just as I needed to know an authentic coin by touch, sight and examination before I could identify a counterfeit, we can't know the truth solely by reading about it. It is only as we spend time relationally with Jesus, in His Word, worship and prayer, and by walking with Him through life, we are certain we can identify a counterfeit. Jesus is truth, and if we are to fully know Him in the depths of our being, we need both the Word and intimate encounters with Him. We need to know not just

who He is, but also how He feels about us and others —
His thoughts and emotions. Truly knowing a person can
never be simply knowing *about* them; we must walk, talk,
laugh and cry with them if we are to truly *know* them. It is
no different with the Lord. He is a person. He made us for
relationship. If we do not know His heart, we cannot
know His mind. When we have the heart of God, we will
have the mind of God. The Tree of Life speaks of this
intimate knowing. It represents the source of Life we
partake in through relationship with the Son of Man, who
is also the Son of God — the Bread of Life, comes through
communion with Jesus. In John 10, Jesus tells the
Pharisees *His sheep will know His voice and will not follow the
voice of a stranger.* This can only happen through intimate
relationship and time together, so His voice can be
discerned from all others. Knowing Him is to know our
Father. You can't help but be a lover once you deeply
partake of Him. In that place, you can't help but love Him
and be transformed to love others.

Several years ago, I got to know an elderly woman
of God. She was a wonderful sister in Christ. She once
asked this question. "Have you ever seen the painting of
Jesus carrying the young sheep on His shoulders?" "Yes,
who hasn't?' I answered. "Do you know why He is
carrying the young sheep on His shoulders?". I thought to
myself, I never really considered it, and answered
"because He loves the sheep". Her answer was incredibly
insightful and powerful. She said, "well yes, He does love
the sheep, however there is more to it. I grew up on a
sheep farm. Sheep are not the smartest animals in the

barn and they will readily hurt themselves by wondering off into dangerous landscapes. There only protection is to be trained to stay near the shepherd and close to home. When there was a young stubborn sheep who kept wandering off my dad, would break a front leg and carefully reset it. Then, while the leg was healing he carried the young sheep on his back. He would tend to it, feed it by hand, and lovingly nurture it back to health. After spending weeks intimately close to his shepherd, the sheep would know the smell, voice, and touch of the shepherd. He would never wander off again." Now, I can't corroborate whether this is what shepherds did in the past, nonetheless, it is a great picture of Jesus, the Good Shepherd, and how he desires to teach us to know His voice, touch, and heart towards us. I do not believe He is the author of pain. I do believe when painful things occur He desires to carry us through, just like the sweet elderly lady's dad did with their sheep when she was a child. He is a tender Father. His highest priority for us is intimate, authentic relationship; to know Him in His fullness.

The Tree of the Knowledge of Good and Evil

As we look at this tree, it is important to understand that man had knowledge of good. Good walked with us in the Garden in the cool of the evening. Good was present when we took our first breath. Good was there with us every day in the Garden. Good is declared before this part of the biblical narrative. Each day of Creation ends with the declaration, *"and it was good.*" When Adam was created, it was declared over him that the Lord's creation of man was very, very good. As I shared in the last chapter, evil also existed prior to Eve eating the apple. Adam and Eve had experiences with good, but had no understanding with evil. What did Satan mean when he said, "God knows you will be like God"? It wasn't a lie. Let's look closely at what comes next. Genesis 3:22 says, "*Then the Lord God said, 'Behold, the man has become like one of us, **knowing good and evil**...'*" We had the opportunity to hold on to our innocence, to be unblemished. We couldn't fully understand good, and we had nothing to compare it to. Now we can tell the difference. We understand the horror of evil and how devastatingly destructive it is. We, like our God, know and experience the catastrophic effects caused by evil let loose. We see the evidence of it all around us. The horrors of evil are unavoidable. In light of this story, the difference between God and man is God understands evil but is not blemished by it. Evil does not touch His goodness and love. For us, it opened the door for our flesh and soul to carry the impulses of darkness. With that act, we shifted from one kingdom to another. From one master and father to another. We traded joy for sorrow, life for death, and love for fear. What is Hell? I believe it is a place completely void of even the smallest particle of love, light, or life. It is a hard thing to consider, a place could exist with no love, no light and nothing life-giving. When we consider this possibility and where we could be because of the Fall, I am thankful that, by His grace, we still have a good measure of love, life, and light here in the present. By His kindness, we are sustained by grace and have a powerful eternal hope—a sure hope in Him. If we are to gain anything from this story, it should be an understanding that we need to run from evil and temptation straight into the arms of the Father and Son.

Chapter 4
Missing the Mark

For the wages of sin is death, but the free gift of God is
eternal life in Christ Jesus our Lord.
Romans 6:23, NLT

Above all, keep loving one another earnestly, since love
covers a multitude of sin. 1 Peter 4:8, ESV

How do we resist sin and the devil and live in love? It
seems easier said than done much of the time, doesn't it?
In Matthew 4:3-4, we see Jesus tempted by Satan in the
wilderness. He had been fasting for forty days and nights.
Jesus was probably starving and near death. We see later
in the story, angels were sent to minister to him. It is safe
to assume he was in very bad shape. Forty days and
nights with nothing to eat? I am a New York boy. I would
be looking for pizza or a good bagel. I would eat almost
anything after 40 days of only water, wouldn't you?

The Bible says, "*The tempter came to him and said, 'If
you are the Son of God, tell these stones to become bread.' Jesus
answered, 'It is written: 'Man shall not live by bread alone, **but***

on every word that comes from the mouth of God.'"
Matthew 4:3-4 (emphasis mine)

Let's dig in and take a closer look. First, the devil
will always tempt you with what you are hungry for. If it
is love, he will tempt you with counterfeit means to attain
it. If a sense of security is what you need, he will tempt
you to go after it by stirring up your insecurity and
causing you to control others. Whatever your fears say
you need, Satan will use to drive you to sin. It may be a
legitimate need, but he will move us to attain it in an
illegitimate way through sin. When I was in Junior High
and High School, I wrestled. In wrestling, as it also is in
certain martial arts, it isn't all about how strong or even
how quick you are. Strength and quickness are incredibly
valuable, but if you can't maintain your balance in the
match, there is a good chance you're going to get thrown
and possibly pinned. I was a decent wrestler, and I was
good with feeling balance. When someone is off balance,
they lean too far, and you use their own body to move
them in the direction it is leaning towards. You don't
resist it; you simply go with it and cause them to continue
in that direction, but in a way they didn't intend. The
enemy wrestles with us in the same way. When we are
bent towards sin in any way, the devil just nudges us a
little further. He simply moves us in the direction we
were leaning but pushes us farther than we intended.
That nudge moves us away from love, towards shame
and fear. Often, this has to do with unresolved fear,
shame, and grief. Remember, fear is the enemy of love;

fear leads us towards sin, shame is a false identity and
unresolved grief can lead us to counterfeit love and peace.
In my case, it was these three that led be to addictive
behaviors.

Defining Sin

The Greek word for sin used in the New Testament
is *hamartia*, which is an archery term meaning *to miss the
mark, to err, to be in error.* To understand this better, we
need to define the mark we are missing. A quick look at
Matthew 5:43-48 will be helpful. In these verses, Jesus is
teaching His disciples about love. In verses 43 and 44,
Jesus says, "*You have heard that it was said, you shall love
your neighbor and hate your enemy. But I say love your
enemies and pray for those who persecute you.*" To some, it
may seem a bit unreasonable. Why should we pray for
our enemies? Verse 45 answers this question with
authority: "*So that you may be sons of your Father in
Heaven.*" Jesus goes on to make it clear how our Father
loves; He makes the sun rise for both the good and the
evil. He sends rain to both the just and unjust. In verse 46,
Jesus makes a statement many have struggled with and
religiosity uses to cause fear, striving, and shame. "*You
therefore must be perfect, as your Heavenly Father is perfect.*"
We have taken this to mean we need to follow the law
perfectly, behave perfectly, we must be perfect in every
way, so we strive to change our behaviors to be holy. This
mindset leaves us striving to make ourselves something
only the Lord can create. The harder we work on
changing our bad behaviors and fail, the more we live

disappointed with ourselves or angry with God. This causes us to live in shame and defeat and act out in unhealthy ways.

Look at the following diagram.

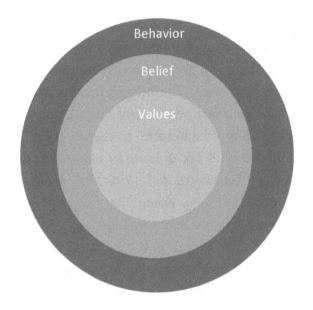

Sin is an internal condition causing certain external behaviors. In dealing with behavioral change, years ago, psychologists learned that if you focus on behavior, people may change by self-discipline for a season, but they have a very high percentage of reverting back to old behaviors. If you change a person's beliefs, they will change their behavior, most likely for a longer season, but a significant percentage will revert. However, if you transform a person's *core values,* what they build their life on, both belief and behavior will have a lasting change. This is most likely why organizations like Alcoholics

Anonymous are relatively successful. The members embrace a core value shift, what they identify as their higher power, this moves them towards lasting change.

Religion tends to focus on beliefs and behaviors. We often think praying the sinner's prayer, or getting converts to go to church, reading their Bible, and even attending weekly meetings will change behavior. Please don't get me wrong. I love to read the Word, and it is foundational to my walk. I love going to church. I am a pastor and believe there's great value in community. In fact, I believe we were made for it, and it is unhealthy not to be in community. Weekly evening meetings, especially Home Group meetings, are incredibly helpful and edifying in our spiritual growth. However, if our core values are not transformed, we tend to walk away, return to old habits, and live with shame, while maintaining facades in order to not be rejected. Unfortunately, there are churches filled with people carrying secret sin, ashamed to bring it forward. All because we don't know how to help people let go and be transformed from the inside out. All too often, we as leaders don't want real transformation. We say we do, but we make no room for the mess that comes with being real. We allow people to stay stuck in a cycle of striving to change their behaviors with little hope. We need to step into true love. We need to be real, vulnerable, and transparent. This brings us back to the definition of sin.

Matthew 5:48 is a hard verse for many of us. It says, "*Be perfect therefore, even as your Heavenly Father is perfect."* How can I possibly be as good as God? I am so far from that reality.

Remember, sin is missing the mark. The mark we miss is *unconditional love.* This love is only accessible by the Holy Spirit. Religion wants you to focus on cleaning up your act and behaving properly. God wants you to focus on being loved and becoming a lover of God and people. In his first letter, the Apostle John tells us, *"We love God because He first loved us."* (1 John 4:1) This transformation in our core is not something we do; it is something the Father, Son, and Holy Spirit do in us. How? As we receive more and more of His love, fear falls away. Jesus is telling us to *love.* Therefore, the mark we miss is the love God is. Sin is missing the mark of unconditional love. Every time we make a choice that is not love, it is sin. When we choose to act in ways hurtful to ourselves, to the Lord or to the people around us, we sin. When we act unlovingly, we sin. That's hard, isn't it? We are a ball of tightly wound emotions, often hard to contain. What is the problem? 1 John 4:16-19 has the key.

*So, we have come to know and to believe the love God has for us. God **IS** love, and whoever abides in love abides in God, and God abides in them. By this is love perfected with us, so that we may have confidence for the day of judgment, because as He is so also, we are in the world. There is **NO** fear in love, but perfect love **(mature, wholehearted, selfless love)** casts out fear. For fear has to do with punishment and whoever fears has not been perfected in love. We love because he has first loved us. (Emphasis mine)*

This is one of my favorite scriptures in the entire Bible. There is so much truth in it. I am going to unwrap it briefly. It deserves more time than we can spend now, it would take another book.

First, we know and believe the love God has for us. It begins with you really believing Jesus, our Father, and Holy Spirit thoroughly and perfectly love you. John makes it easier when he says, *"God IS love."* When I speak at conferences, I often like to say to the people gathered, "God is NOT a loving God." I wait for what seems like a long time and watch the audience as their faces start to say, "Is this guy crazy?" Pastors start to give me a look that questions their own intelligence for inviting me in. I slowly say, very precisely, "No, God is NOT a loving God, God IS love. He is the substance of love, the essence of love. There is no place in the universe where true love can be experienced without Him being present. Of course, He is loving, because love requires expressions that demonstrate love." I quote Paul in Acts 17 when he addresses the Athenians, *"And in Him you live and move and have your very being."* You are saturated, immersed, breathing in and out the God who IS love. He loves you thoroughly, completely, perfectly. You were made from love, for love, to be loved, and to demonstrate His love. You can't escape Him, and therefore, you cannot escape love. But, you can deny it, reject it, run away from it, and be lost without it. That is on you, not on the God who is love. Isn't that a simple yet amazing revelation?

So, what is the problem? FEAR! Fear is the problem. We all have heard it said the opposite of love is... HATE. No, the opposite of love is fear. Sin drives us to fear, and fear drives everything else. All our ills on the planet are derived from fear. What is shame? Fear. What is anxiety? Fear. What is racism? Fear. What causes abortion? Fear. Fear is the enemy's currency. Why is fear so powerful against us? Because we still think we are punishable. Fear was the byproduct of the fall. Adam and Eve's response to God was shame. Shame is fear that says, "I AM something wrong." It is a lying identity. It is a destroyer. For a short time a few years ago, I met with students who were part of the campus Christian club at a college near me. One day, I asked about a dozen of them, "Are you saints or sinners?" They looked at me, unwilling to answer, knowing I was probably setting them up. One very bright young man, a leader in the group and the son of a pastor, confidently spoke out, "We are sinners." I said, "Really? Where does the Bible say we are sinners?" He said, "Paul said, 'We are sinners saved by grace.'" "Yes," I said. "But it says *saved*, past tense. So, if we are saved, are we now sons and daughters, or sinners?" Time had ended, so I let him off the hook and encouraged them all to consider this: "If Jesus died to take on our sin—all our sin—and be punished, are we still punishable?" You see, that is the problem. Many of us have not resolved this issue in our hearts. In our heads and in our theology, we may say Jesus died for my sin. But because we have not fully come to experience and know the *fullness* of our Father's love for us in Christ, when we blow it, we fear we will be punished. Don't get me wrong, I know we wrestle with sin, and sometimes sin wins, but we aren't to be punished, we are to repent. If we, who have given our life to Christ, are still punishable, Jesus' sacrifice on the Cross was not sufficient, and that just is NOT true. It was completely and perfectly sufficient. Will you believe? In the scripture above, John starts with saying, *"We know **and** believe the love, the God who is love, has for us..."* It is not enough to know the information; you must have the knowing experience in your heart and believe it. It is through intimate, experiential times with Holy Spirit that drive this home, along with the Word.

When I was first growing in understanding the Father's love, there was a time I had a real crisis. I felt a lot of shame, and it was crippling me. I was a worship leader and small group leader. My wife was the children's ministry director, and we were just two years into a church plant. People looked to me as a leader and some as their pastor. On the outside, I seemed to have it all together. The inside was quite another story, and I was riddled with shame. I was led by a leader who was a good man, but broken, and I was very fearful of him. I often felt like I was under a microscope. The feeling of fear and shame caused me to do some things out of insecurity that made things worse, causing me to sin, to miss the mark of love. I felt I couldn't do anything right, and it was just a matter of time before the axe would fall. As a result, I questioned whether God really loved me. After all, it seemed I couldn't do anything right, and I had a lot of anxiety I kept hidden under false confidence. I felt lonely, with no one I could trust to share it with. All I could do was cry to the Lord, "Do You love me? Are You there?

Help me. I am unworthy!" One Sunday, we had a guest couple come and share. When they were done, they invited people up for ministry. Usually during ministry, I would sing or lead worship while others ministered. Sometimes I would minister, but rarely did I receive ministry. Receiving ministry would require vulnerability. This day, I went up and stood there. I was fine if no one came to pray. In fact, I preferred it. Thankfully, no one did. I stood there as His presence was on me, and I gently wept. I said, "Father, do You love me? Jesus, do You love me?" Over and over, I begged for an answer that would take my fear away. Suddenly, softly, I heard in my heart the same words the Lord had asked me a few years earlier. I was on my way to work—my son, Jason, wasn't quite two years old—and the Lord said to me, "Do you love me?" "Yes, I love You," I replied. He asked if I loved Him enough to give Him my only son. I broke and wept. "Yes, I love You enough to give you my son." Less than a week later, Jason was in the hospital with a rare disease known as Kawasaki's. Thankfully, the Lord saved him, but it became a defining moment for Patti, Jason, and I in our walk with God, growing to trust Him in all things.

So, here I was, once again struggling with my self-worth and questioning His love for me. Again, He asked me the same question. This time, He was about to reveal something I had not understood. He was going to drive home the reality of His love for me. "Phill, do you love Me?" "Yes Lord, I love You," I replied. "It is impossible for you to love Me without Me first loving you. If you know you love Me, you must rest in the knowledge that I love you." He took 1 John 4:19, *"We love because He first loved us,"* and used it to drive home the reality of His love for me. Though I may stumble, I can rest in Him because I now understand His love. Ever since then, I have not questioned my Father's love for me. I've had pockets of shame and doubt to process through, but I know those are just lies, and I declare His love over myself.

Defining Love

Since we have defined and unwrapped sin, and talked a lot about love, it seems worthwhile to clearly unwrap the God-love we are to walk in. In an earlier chapter, I shared that human love is expectation, which leads to exploitation—using people, knowingly or unknowingly—to meet our own need. When there is resistance or the expectation is unmet, we begin to demand our needs be met, often by subtle and sometimes not so subtle manipulation. What we are doing is exercising the power of control. Most often, our unknown motive for this behavior is fear, rejection, or past hurt. At the core, it is selfish pride. This destroys the foundation of love needed to strengthen the very relationships we most value. We end up sabotaging our most important relationships—the ones we need most to feel safe.

In 1 Corinthians 13, the Apostle Paul gives us a brilliant picture of what love is and isn't.

"Love is patient and kind; love does NOT envy or boast; it is NOT arrogant or rude. It does NOT insist on its own way; it is NOT irritable or resentful; it does NOT rejoice at

wrongdoing, but rejoices with the truth. Love bears ALL things, believes ALL things, hopes ALL things, endures ALL things. Love NEVER ends." 1 Corinthians 13:4-8a, ESV (emphasis mine)

It is important to understand this love is without conditions. We can say we do not have expectations for people, but we live it out by being distant and detached. That would not be love; it would be fear. Love engages people. Love moves us towards connection and relationship. When Paul lists the "nots," he is showing us how we generally act towards each other. He is saying that is not what love is. It isn't being envious when others are blessed, instead of being happy and joyful for them. I often hear people say, "Look, so-and-so just got a new dining room set, car, big screen TV. They always complain about not having money, but they bought a new... Well, that's okay." The *"that's okay"* is a veiled attempt to hide envy. Envy comes from a pauper spirit telling us "others get more than me." It somehow feels like another person's blessing takes away from ours. Many people are not aware of this attitude; sin has programmed them this way since childhood. Arrogance is insecurity manifesting as a superior attitude. Generally, people with a superiority complex are fearful they don't measure up, so they overcompensate. This is at the heart of arrogance. Arrogance is a form of pride. Arrogant people are often rude, putting others down to build themselves up. Love isn't controlling, and it doesn't demand its own way. A person walking in love isn't short tempered or easily irritated. They don't feel the need to defend themselves, in part because when they are wrong, they take responsibility and act lovingly to restore relationship. Love doesn't love to receive love in return. Love is its own reward. Jesus didn't love so people would love Him. I am sure He appreciated and trusted those who loved Him, but He didn't need their love to love them in return. He loved them because He was and is a lover. That is what He calls us to. Again, loving is its own reward. I love my wife, my sons, my daughter-in-love, my friends, and church. I don't love them because they love me. I love them simply because I do, because I have been commanded to. It is what my Father desires. One of the primary ways we demonstrate our obedience to God is by acting in love. Loving others should become our passion because we want to be like Him, and we want to please Him - not to earn love, but rather from love. This realization empowers us to need nothing from people to love them. It is powerful, and it changes peoples' lives — your own and those around you.

If we start to understand the power we have, we begin to realize love is not an emotion. Yes, it can be very emotional at times, but the foundation of love is choice. I can choose to love or not. It is my choice. It is your choice. Choosing to act lovingly, selflessly, is what love is and more. It is powerful beyond our understanding. It is more powerful than all the atomic bombs that have ever existed. Love is what holds the universe together. It is in the most microcosmic particles of existence, and it fills the Heavens. Because Love is a living being, the Maker of

Heaven and Earth, the Eternal Father, the Everlasting Son, The King of Kings and Lord of Lords, the Spirit of Life, Love is powerful, real, and alive. When we love well, we make Him known beyond words. He becomes tangible in us and through us. You are powerful when you live your life this way.

Whatever you fix your eyes and heart on will be the place of life for you; it will be what brings light to your life. It will be what forms your concept of love and the way you love. Fix your eyes on Jesus and have life everlasting, joy abundant, faith without measure, hope overflowing.

Worship and Life

I am the Lord Your God, who brought you out of Egypt, out of the land of slavery. You shall have no other gods before me. Deuteronomy 5:6-7, NIV

Away from me Satan! For it is written: "Worship the Lord your God, and serve him only. Matthew 4:10, NIV

The Lord is my light and my salvation; whom shall I fear? The Lord is the stronghold of my life; of whom shall I be afraid? Psalm 27:1, NIV

Why do we worship God? Why do we sing songs to Him? Why must we acknowledge Him always? Why? Does He need affirmation of our love to feel loved? One reason we worship God, the triune God, is because He alone is worthy to be praised. He deserves the honor, glory, and praise. He flat out deserves it. It's that simple. However, there is another very important reason. We were made to worship. It is in our spiritual DNA to worship. All humans worship something or someone; it is unavoidable. We have been worshipping since we had breath breathed into us.

"The chief end of man is to glorify God, and to enjoy Him forever." The Westminster Shorter Catechism

To glorify God and to worship Him are inseparable. In our church culture, when we mention worship, we immediately think of a worship service or singing worship music. I love both. I love to sing praises to the Lord, and I love to sing intimate love songs to my Savior. When His presence comes, it is the sweetest time. Worship is a powerful tool to shift atmospheres as the Lord is enthroned upon the praise and worship of His children. However, if this is the complete definition and expression of worship, we have missed it. We are to glorify God in all of life. What does that mean? I believe it means when all we do, when every part of our life is lived out and expressed in a way that pleases Him and points people towards Him, we glorify Him. When we reveal, with love in action, the goodness, kindness, and love of God, we glorify Him. When we put our religion aside and accurately represent His heart, we glorify Him. When we step out to heal the sick in Jesus' name, when we minister deliverance and inner healing, we glorify Him. We also glorify Him when we put love in action with a sick neighbor, grieving friend, or stranger. When we feed the poor, visit those in jail, or simply listen to a broken heart, we glorify Him. Ultimately, when we love people with His love, with His heart, we glorify Him. I believe it was St. Francis of Assisi who said, "Preach the gospel to everyone, and when necessary, use words." I love that. When our life is the message that declares the good news, we glorify God. Glorifying Him is our whole life. Every part of it is for His glory.

I love the second part of the chief end of man: *enjoy Him forever*. We are not talking about enjoying a good movie or party, or even a good conversation with a dear friend. Not even enjoying your spouse or children, all wonderful gifts to be enjoyed. But to be *in joy with God,* to live forever in a state of joy with the One who is the source of perfect joy? I can't begin to fully comprehend that. The truly wonderful thing is we get to have access to joy in good measure on this side of eternity, and perfectly on the other side. Jesus said in John 15:11, *"These things I have spoken to you that my joy may be in you, and that your joy may be full,"* and in John 16:24, *"Ask, and you will receive, that your joy may be full."* Joy is one of the most profound expressions of life. Worship, in all forms, draws us to the Lord. We may weep or we may laugh, but the Lord desires we live in joy. It is the first fruit of the Spirit mentioned after love. In my experience, joy and peace come in tandem. You can't have joy and not have the peace of God. You can't have His peace and not walk in joy. Fixing our eyes on the Lord in all circumstances, with hope, in faith, is an act of worship. We are saying, "You are the One I value above all things. I know You are faithful and true. I trust in You." That is worship. It glorifies God and brings joy and peace.

Shouldn't we feel joyful all the time? If there was ever a loaded question, this may be it. What do you mean by 'feel'? When most people think of joy, they think of an emotion, like happy. We erroneously think happiness means joyfulness and vice versa. Happiness is an external, emotional state. Happy feelings come and go. If our joy is in our happy feelings, we are going to be on a very frustrating and unfulfilling rollercoaster. Remember, *"We walk by faith and not by sight."* We don't live life out of our emotions. Living this way is a sure-fire recipe for an unstable, fear-based life. No, we live our life with confidence in the goodness and kindness of God. We live a worshipful life trusting in His heart for us. This lifestyle brings His love to life in our inner man, and one of the byproducts is joy. Joy is an expression of hope that can't be shaken. It is an inner condition of the life of the Spirit. It is powerful and a key indicator we are filled with life.

In conclusion, a worshipful lifestyle empowers us to receive and flow with His life. We develop this lifestyle through personal, intimate worship, meditating on His Word, a consistent, intimate prayer life, and loving, active service. Let me add one note regarding prayer. There are many types of prayer, and they are all fruitful. However, prayer that sustains intimacy looks very much like intimate communication with a loved one. It is conversational and not always formal. It is sharing your heart, hopes, desires, fears and joys, asking questions, listening, and agreeing with the Lord. It is deep friendship communicated with your Father. It can be done unceasingly. This is the relationship-building prayer you participate in while doing life with the Father, Son, and Holy Spirit. Don't get me wrong—we also need to be engaged in intercession, but prayer needs to flow from fellowship with God.

Section Three

Two Fathers

and Two Kingdoms

Chapter 5
The Father of Lies

You are of your father the devil, and your will is to do your father's desires. He was a murderer from the beginning, and does not stand in the truth, because there is no truth in him. When he lies, he speaks out of his own character, for he is a liar and the father of lies. John 8:44, ESV

In chapter one, we spoke about the role of a father. We saw how fathers, by God's design, have been uniquely entrusted and empowered with the role of communicating identity. We also defined identity as "the distinctive qualities of a thing that makes it unique from all others of its kind." So, in simple terms, *identity* is our personal individuality that makes us unique from all other humans. However, by nature, identity is not something we can define on our own. Within identity, there are several layers. One layer is defined by how we are loved and accepted. The issue is whether we believe we are perfectly loved by our Father. The problem is never, does God love us? It is always, do we believe He loves us, and loves us perfectly? Therefore, identity is defined by the One who made us. Identity says I belong. I am valuable. I have a reason, a purpose, and I am designed to be the only one like me. That is powerful. No longer do we compete with others out of fear of not getting what we want or need. No, we love and like who we are, and we are not threatened by nor do we need to be a threat to others. Why? Because they, too, are uniquely made to be who they are, to carry the gifts and talents in their unique mix. It is a win-win, and it is how we were made. A heart steadfast in its identity releases honor and magnifies love.

I grew up with friends who were identical twin brothers, Mickey and Lenny. The only difference was Lenny was maybe a half inch taller and just a little broader. If you knew them well, you could tell who was who. If you didn't, you wouldn't know who you were talking to. As teenagers, this was sometimes fun, especially in fooling teenage girls. Both brothers were athletic, pretty good students, and had similar likes and talents. However, they also had unique personalities, opinions, and thoughts. They were attracted to different women. The way they engaged people was different, and how people viewed them was different. Mick was very outgoing and made a lot of friends, while Len was a little more reserved. My point is that as much as they were identical twins, it was mainly in outward appearance and not in the core of who they are. God intended it that way. We can be similar, but never the same. He made every one of us unique.

So what is the problem? Why do we fear so many things, and struggle the way we do? We have an enemy that understands how powerful we will be when we understand who we are: the very children of the living God. In the Garden of Eden, we were made orphans by the choices our forefather and mother made. They didn't fully understand the ramifications of their rebellion. They didn't understand their choice would devastate creation in ways they could not perceive. They didn't understand how fatherlessness would open the door to an evil, surrogate father. When they agreed with a lie about our Father, they repositioned man under the Father of Lies, a brutal usurper who hates us as much as he hates his creator. Ever since then, we have been on a journey back to the Father.

Unwrapping John 8:12-58

In many ways, the Gospel of John is as much the gospel of the Father as it is the gospel of Jesus. In John chapter 8, there is a discourse between Jesus and the Pharisees. It serves as a fascinating window into how the enemy assaults identity and how we should stand in our true identity. Starting in verse 12, Jesus says, "*I am the light of the world.*" The Pharisees hear this and make an interesting statement in verse 13. The Pharisees said to Him, "*You are bearing witness about yourself; your testimony is not true.*" Jesus starts with an "I am" statement. "I am" statements are identity statements. When we say "I am," we are defining who or what we are. The Pharisees question Jesus' truth claims, because to do so and prove Him a liar would destroy His testimony. Their claim is a legal one. Jesus is the only one saying it, and there are no witnesses; it is therefore false. Jesus responds in verse 18, "*I am the one who bears witness about myself, and the Father who sent me bears witness about me.*" He brings His Father into it and brings the debate to a new level. He is saying, "I can bear witness as to who I am because my Father says the same thing about me." His Father defines His identity. By the way, this is also true for us; our Father in Christ defines us as well. How awesome!

The Pharisees challenge Him, "Where is your father? Show us your father. Where is your proof?" Jesus brings them in with His response, *"You don't know me and neither do you know my Father. If you knew me, you would know my Father."* I get excited when I read this because Jesus is about to reveal to them, and to us, something no one understood before. He is about to reveal the foundation of religiosity; the question of who we serve. This conversation is the reason they had to execute Him. Stay with me.

In verses 12-20, Jesus creates the dispute over His testimony about who He is — His identity. In verses 21-30, the Pharisees start to dispute it.

*He said to them, "You are from below; I am from above. You are of this world; I am not of this world. I told you that you would die in your sins, for unless you believe that **I am he** you will die in your sins." So they said to him, "Who are you?" Jesus said to them, "Just what I have been telling you from the beginning..." So Jesus said to them, "When you have lifted up the Son of Man, then you will know that **I am he**, and that I do nothing on my own authority, but speak just as the Father taught me."*

Jesus is pressing the point. He makes two more identity statements. The Pharisees know full well He is saying, *"I am My Father's Son."* He is reinforcing who He is, and as He affirms His identity, those watching believe Him. At the same time, He is making an identity statement about them. *"You are from below; I am from above. You are of this world; I am not of this world."* He is setting them up for the climax, the slam dunk, the in-your-face moment of this debate. By stating where He is from, contrasting it with where they are from, He is clarifying why they are blind to the truth. Continuing, Jesus says, *"When you have lifted up the Son of Man, then you will know that **I am he**, and that I do nothing on my own authority, but speak just as the Father taught me."*

In verses 31-47, it all starts to come together.

> *"If you abide in my word, you are truly my disciples, and you will know the truth, and the truth will set you free."*
> They answered him, *"We are offspring of Abraham and have never been enslaved to anyone. How is it that you say, 'You will become free'?"*

Their response, *"We are offspring of Abraham and have never been enslaved to anyone,"* displays the revelation Jesus was working towards. This is foundational to understanding this chapter. They have now identified themselves with their religion and tradition, but not with God. Jesus does not refute it; He clarifies it. Jesus has been talking about a spiritual and eternal identity — something superior to the natural family lineage we are born into. He is pointing to the fact that ultimately it is God who defines us, not our natural lineage or our traditions. It doesn't matter what your natural lineage is, true life comes from your spiritual life. Their argument that they are Abraham's children has now moved to authority. Jesus has been saying the things He says and teaches have the authority of His Father, God.

"We have one Father — even God." Jesus said to them, "If God were your Father, you would love me, for I came from God and I am here. I came not of my own accord, but he sent me. Why do you not understand what I say? It is because you cannot bear to hear my word. You are of your father the devil, and your will is to do your father's desires. He was a murderer from the beginning, and does not stand in the truth, because there is no truth in him. When he lies, he speaks out of his own character, for he is a liar and the father of lies." John 8:41-44

For the first time in all the scripture, Jesus reveals Satan as the usurping father. Don't misunderstand me; there is nothing fatherly about him. He is more like someone who kidnaps a child, convinces them he is their father, and proceeds to abuse, manipulate, and imprison them in fear. Jesus continues to press the point of who He is until they are filled with rage and pick up stones to kill him.

This opens a whole new understanding of how the enemy has impacted man. Jesus is identifying the Pharisees as offspring of the devil. His words seem harsh.

He is leaving no room for doubt as to who He is, what He came for, and that the only way to the Father is through Him. He is also establishing who Satan is and how he works against man. Their argument at the very beginning questions His authority; by what and whose authority do you say and do what you do? He has made it all perfectly clear — by the authority in me as a Son of the Father. At the same time, He is saying, "By what authority do you stand here to challenge me? Your actions and words clearly show you are not of God. If you were, you would receive me. Therefore, you are from the devil." Everyone watching was left with a clear decision — believe or not believe.

In terms of our conversation, Jesus opens the door of understanding the importance of knowing who you are and where you come from — your true identity. Jesus tells us the enemy has been redefining our individual and corporate identity since the Garden. It has always been part of his plan to keep the ones who bear the *imago Dei* in bondage.

The Father of Lies — The Devil at the Fall

If we look closely at Genesis 3, we see a conversation between the serpent and Eve. It mirrors the conversation that took place between Jesus and the Pharisees.

He said to the woman, "Did God actually say, 'You shall not eat of any tree in the garden'?" And the woman said to the serpent, "We may eat of the fruit of the trees in the garden, but God said, 'You shall not eat of the fruit of the tree that is in the midst of the garden, neither shall you touch it, lest you die.'"

We have looked at these verses in detail earlier. Now, I want us to look at them in terms of the type of conversation that ensues and how it parallels to what we just read in John 8. Both conversations start with a question. Both are questioning authority, and both are questioning the Father. In John 8, the Pharisees are blatantly questioning the authority of Jesus and who His Father is. In Genesis 3, it is an indirect question. By asking, "Did God really say?", the serpent is attacking the Father's integrity—His trustworthiness. These are two things Kingdom authority sits on. God's authority comes from the reality that every word from His mouth is truth, and He has perfect integrity. *"Righteousness and justice are the foundation of your throne," Psalm 89:14.* This verse tells us God's authority sits on His perfect rightness, integrity, faithfulness, and trustworthiness; these are rooted in His perfect love. The serpent caused Eve to question God's integrity and trustworthiness, and in doing so, he provokes her to question her relationship with her maker. The devil tried to do the same with Jesus in the wilderness, and now the Pharisees are attempting the same with the question, "In whose authority?" In all these cases, the devil, the "Father of Lies," is assaulting our identity and God's integrity. It is his favorite tactic, his ploy—to separate our heart from God's, move us towards fear and restlessness, and keep us from the *knowledge of*

God. Why? Because identity is spoken into a person by one in authority. As a father, I was given authority for a season, to train my children up. In that authority, I was to father them in such a way they would be able to identify with Father God and Jesus in a healthy way. At the same time, I spoke their true identities into them, until the time they could walk in the authority of being His sons. You cannot separate identity and authority. In the Kingdom, His power, the power of the Holy Spirit, most fully flows through children who know He is their Father and are confident in His goodness, kindness, and love for them and for people.

The Identity from the Father of Lies

The effect of false identities sowed into man through the fall has been devastating. While there are many false identities, they all flow out of two spirits—the orphan spirit and the pauper spirit. I am not saying every human has a demon called the orphan or pauper spirit. What I am saying is after the Fall, the primary spiritual influence Satan has been sowing in humanity is identities as orphans and paupers. Nevertheless, in some cases of deliverance ministry, I have literally broken the power of the orphan spirit and the pauper spirit, commanded them to leave, and the individual receiving ministry said it felt like something left them; a weight came off them.

The Orphan Spirit

Ever since Adam and Eve, the orphan spirit has permeated the planet, wreaking havoc everywhere. I

believe most of our struggles are a result of the influence
of this spirit in our lives. When we fell from grace, our
great loss was relationship with our maker, our Father.
We became orphaned. To some degree, every human has
experienced a sense of abandonment, loneliness,
aloneness, alienation, and isolation. My father-in-law, one
of my best friends, suffered terrible depression until the
day the Lord took him home at age 64. I also had a good
friend whom I worked for, who suffered from depression.
They both went through it at the same time. This gave me
an up close and personal view, as I would counsel both
through it at times. For a while, I asked the Lord, "What is
the root cause of depression?" One day, quite
unexpectedly, I heard Him say, "Abandonment. The fear
of abandonment is the root of depression." I know
professionals may have a different opinion. They might
point to trauma, an issue of heredity, or chemical
imbalance. I believe the Lord. As I have watched others
over the years, I do believe the spiritual core to depression
is the fear of abandonment coming with an orphan spirit.
There are all different reasons people have this fear, and it
can remain unknown, or hidden. We may see rejection,
abuse, and many other valid and understandable reasons
for depression, even heredity. But, at the core, depression
is Satan's lie that God abandoned humanity, though in
truth we rejected our Heavenly Father. Satan stole us
from Him. The first indication of sin was blame-shifting.
"The serpent made me," or "The woman You gave me
made me..." You have to love Adam; he actually tried to

blame God. We live in a lie that God is distant, uncaring, and punitive. This couldn't be further from the truth.

> *"I believe all of the emotional, physical and spiritual ills of society can be traced to humans feeling alienated from God and their biological fathers."* Joseph Mattera, Charisma News

Alienated! Feeling estranged, isolated, abandoned — could that be the root cause of most, if not all, our ills? I believe it very well may be.

I once read, "An orphan spirit will tend to mix grace with sin and rule keeping." I don't remember where I read it, but it is the truth. Because orphans are always afraid they will be kicked out of the Father's house, they are afraid they will never measure up to earn love and have safety. The orphan spirit causes us to strive. Grace cannot be mixed with sin because sin kills; grace brings life *(James 1:14-15)*. Grace cannot be mixed with the law through "performance," because it makes grace ineffectual *(Galatians 2:21)*. We are all unique; the influence, effects, and working out of the orphan spirit can be different for each of us. It is more obvious in some than others. Many who have been raised in a good and loving family will demonstrate less of its effect. Others from severely broken homes will most likely demonstrate the impact more profoundly. From my personal experience and in ministry, I have never run into anyone who hasn't carried something of this spirit at some point in their life. As believers, we received the spirit of adoption and are moving towards complete freedom. Many have been completely freed, although it is a process. I have traveled for five years teaching churches and parachurch organizations about these spirits. I have seen countless people set free from the orphan spirit and its influence. I have routinely heard things like, "I can't believe how much inner healing I received from this message and the ministry that followed. I am freer now, after just a weekend, than I have been in years of prayer and counseling." My traveling mate, Dan, and I could tell you story after story of testimonies. Once the orphan spirit is broken and you come to know the Father's love, it's like someone turned the lights on for the first time in your life. Simply amazing!

Besides abandonment, isolation, loneliness, aloneness, and alienation, the common characteristics of the orphan spirit are insecurity, anxiety, terror, unreasonable fears, jealousy, envy, mistrust, suspicion, fear of man, fear of failure, fear of losing loved ones, expecting rejection, and depression. An orphan spirit keeps us from understanding grace because an orphan believes nothing comes easily. An orphan is always working to be loved and expects not to be good enough in the end. Grace doesn't make sense to an orphan. There are countless believers, our brothers and sisters, who are still in bondage to this spirit through religiosity, striving through works and following lists of rules. They can't enjoy and rest in the perfect love provided through the grace that comes with the spirit of adoption, because religious systems still require they follow the rules. Often, this mindset appears very subtly in things like, if you just pray more, study more, come to church more, give more, do more, you will... It is a trap. Remember, religion is always about behavior and homogeny, in which being a good Christian demands you look like us, talk like us, and behave like us, and then you will be fine. Religion always moves us to conformity and away from transformation. Why? Because conformity is external, and transformation is internal; it is in our core that transformation happens. By teaching us to focus on conforming what we look like and act like on the outside, we are kept from the surrender that causes transformation of our inner man. There is freedom with the Lord. The orphan spirit keeps us believing we aren't home yet; we can still be lost. We have the freedom to choose to walk away, but we will never be abandoned by God.

The Pauper Spirit

The pauper spirit is similar to the orphan spirit. While the orphan spirit impacts relationships, how you see yourself, and how you perceive people see you, the pauper spirit is primarily focused on the areas of provision, position, and purpose. They function as a pair. They jumped in on the curse and placed man in bondage to these fears.

To the woman He said, "I will greatly multiply your pain in childbirth, in pain you will bring forth children; Yet your desire will be for your husband, And he will rule over you."

"Because you have listened to the voice of your wife, and have eaten from the tree about which I commanded you, saying, 'You shall not eat from it'; **Cursed is the ground because of you; In toil you will eat of it all the days of your life.** *"Both thorns and thistles it shall grow for you; And you will eat the plants of the field; By the sweat of your face you will eat bread, till you return to the ground, because from it you were taken; For you are dust, and to dust you shall return." Genesis 3:16-19, NASB (emphasis mine)*

There is so much in here that helps us understand the impact of the Fall, as well as how Satan has used it to place us in bondage and keep us there. Most often, we've read this as God's wrath and judgment on man. I invite you to see it from a different angle. What if our Father wasn't cursing us? What if He was telling us what we had just opened ourselves up to, and how our choice was not just going to impact man personally, but also the planet? Stay with me. Let's unwrap this further.

Let's look at the words to Adam. He listened to his wife instead of being obedient to the Lord. Because he chose his wife over God, the ground was cursed. What does that mean? Before Adam rebelled, the ground produced without needing to be tended to. Everything needed came forth naturally, without man's care. The ground, by God's design, provided sustenance. The Father provided all that was needed. Adam had no knowledge of toil, hard work and sweat, or the frustration of failed crops, or dying, non-producing cattle. Hunger was foreign to man. Everything they needed for each day was built into the Father's creation. His grace was everywhere to be found. God explains, "Your decision to turn from Me and go your own way means you now have to work to sustain yourself. You couldn't see all I was providing for you. Now you must labor for what was provided without cost. You are now responsible to provide for your wife and children until the day you die and return to the ground. This is what you have brought upon yourself and your offspring. I didn't do this to you; you did this to yourself. You wanted to be like God, I am the self-sustaining One. Now you must work to sustain yourself and your family, because you chose to separate yourself from Me."

God designed the universe in such a way grace would flow from relational intimacy; continuous connection with our Father. He provides grace for everything we need, to sustain our body, soul, and spirit. Worship is the means to connection and intimacy with God as our source for life. When I say worship, I am not talking about singing songs. I am speaking about a lifestyle that has a loving relationship with the triune God in the center of all we are and do. When intimacy is broken, relational separation with the One who is life for us is broken, grace is hindered, and with it, life — relationally and physically, in our soul and spirit. Without His life, our experience is death in varied forms. When my wife and I are disconnected, when we are not loving each other well, we hinder the life we share that brings joy to our relationship. Our life, as one flesh, experiences death. If we do not restore love, the inevitable is a broken relationship resulting in relational death—divorce. I am thankful that after nearly 40 years of marriage, we love each other more now than ever. When mankind separated from God, His life-sustaining provision was hindered by our sin. In His kindness, He provided the means of sustaining grace to us from before the foundation of the world through Christ *(Ephesians 1:4-6 and Revelation 13:8)*. Yet, we still experienced death from a broken relationship with God.

After the Fall, Adam, the first created and appointed one, carried the weight and responsibility of providing for his family in all the natural ways his Heavenly Father provided before the Fall. This did not include only physical needs, but also headship. Remember, Adam and Eve's relationship before the Fall was not hierarchal. They were one flesh; she was his perfect helpmate. They were perfectly complimentary. Their relationship was in priority order in function, not in authority. As you will see, the Fall shifted things.

Eve carried another set of consequences, unique to the feminine and equally destructive. *"In pain, you will bring forth children;* **Yet your desire will be for your husband, and he will rule over you."** First, she would have great pain in childbirth. Before this, it seems as though childbirth was relatively painless. Every woman wishes they could get that back. Second, and this is profound, her desire would be for her husband, and he would rule over her. What does this mean? The word desire used here in Hebrew is *teshuqah*. Most translations have applied it to mean desire. However, it is an obscure

100

word that only appears three times in scripture. We see it here, in Genesis 4:7, and in Song of Solomon 7:12. This word can also mean longing and turning. Whichever way we interpret it, the application is relevant to all. The Lord is declaring over Eve, "You will desire, long for, and turn towards your husband to meet all your needs, and He will now rule over you." Let us be clear, the Lord is not saying He is declaring that men "are to rule" over women. He is saying this is what is going to happen because of your choice, Eve. The woman will now look to the man to provide her with all the Lord provided in the Garden: provision, self-worth, purpose, safety, and security; all that is needed for a healthy body and soul. In this way, man will rule over her, as he takes the role previously filled for her by the Lord. This is the battle of the sexes. On the other side, man toils for provision and needs the woman to give him what he has lost: love, intimacy, deep friendship, respect, affirmation, affection, and self-worth.

What does this mean in context of the pauper spirit? As I said, the orphan and pauper spirit are similar and travel together. The pauper spirit causes us to fear there will never be enough. It influences people to think there is only so much of the pie to go around, and there isn't enough for me. It often breeds a competitive spirit for fear someone else will get our share. Envy, covetousness, and jealousy are effects of this spirit. This spirit sees other people as a threat to getting what you want and need. It says things like, "I will never have a nice home, enough money to retire, or a new car," and so on. It equates lack with the absence of love. God must not love me; if He did, I wouldn't struggle financially. Or, He must love them more because look at all they have. Men might feel like they can't earn enough, like someone always gets more. In a woman, this fear often demands the husband get a better job. With the majority of women working today, they, too, can carry the same fears that were traditionally on men.

The fear of lack is a terrible and crippling fear. Jesus addresses this in Matthew 6:19-20. Jesus teaches not to store up treasures here on earth where they will wither away and be destroyed. Instead, store up eternal treasures in Heaven. In verse 21, Jesus says, *"For where your treasure is, there your heart will be also."* This is the fight we engage in when we deal with this spirit. When fear of lack is the state of our heart, we seek after treasures on earth, instead of trusting God and storing up treasures in Heaven. In the next several verses, Jesus describes the door: the eyes. Your eyes, the eyes of your heart, will focus on what you treasure and what you value. Where your treasure is, your heart will be. I like to say it this way: what you fix your eyes on, what your heart desires, will become the object of your worship. It is subtle; we don't realize it, but what drives us is what we are seeking to get life from. Jesus says we cannot serve two masters. *"Either you will hate the one and love the other, or you will be devoted to the one and despise the other. You cannot serve both God and mammon,"* *Mathew 6:24.*

Mammon, in its simplest terms, is lust for wealth. It is an idol of materialism. The pauper spirit opens us up to the influence of mammon. I have heard people say, "I am not materialistic. I don't have expensive things." Having material things and being driven by mammon are not the same thing. Envy of what others have, this fear of lack drives us to anxiety, and stinginess as opposed to generosity — these all speak of mammon. Mammon is of the pauper spirit. Mammon always works in fear, anxiety, and striving. This can either be internal striving, externally striving for more, or most often, both. If this is what drives you, you will never be satisfied with what you have. You will never have "enough." This will be a wall between you and your understanding and experience of your Father's love.

Chapter 6
Overcoming the Orphan
and Pauper Spirits

For though we live in the world, we do not wage war as the world does. The weapons we fight with are not the weapons of the world. On the contrary, they have divine power to demolish strongholds. We demolish arguments and every pretension that sets itself up against the knowledge of God, and we take captive every thought to make it obedient to Christ. 2 Corinthians 10:3-5, NIV

Every born-again believer has the Holy Spirit indwelling their spirit. The role of the Holy Spirit is to teach and empower our spirit to take authority over our flesh and soul, empowering us to live by the Spirit. We are being prepared to rule and reign at the side of our Elder Brother, Lord of Lords, Mighty King, Savior and Friend, Jesus. As we learn to walk in His love, authority, and power, we overcome the influence of both the orphan and pauper spirit. They have manipulated our thoughts and emotions, creating strongholds—ways of thinking and feeling—that war internally against the truth of who our Father is and how He feels towards His beloved children. I have found, in my 35 years of pursuing and walking with the One my soul loves, when there is a lie, especially one influenced by a demonic stronghold, Jesus generally wants me to overcome it by the power of His Spirit, with faith, tenacity, and perseverance. Why? From what I have experienced, there are two main reasons. He wants me to enjoy the victory I have through Him. It builds me up in faith and confidence in the authority I have in Him. He also wants me to know this truth, with Him, "All things are possible," because "He who is in me is greater than he who is in the world," and, "I am more than a conqueror through Christ Jesus." I am a prince, a little king, a victor in Christ, a fearless warrior, a lover of God and people; I am His son. That is powerful. Through this process, He is preparing us to rule as His family. This is an amazing truth. The second reason is what you overcome gives you authority to set others free from the same bondage. It is one of the ways He works all things for good.

We walk through this process in partnership with Holy Spirit by faith. Faith flows from trust, resting in His trustworthiness to do all He says He will do. Faith is the assurance, the guarantee of what we hope for; it flows from confidence that His heart is to give us what we hope for when it lines up with His heart. It rests in Jesus, the perfect truth. It is all relational. We all have been broken. I have been as broken as anyone. I almost died at birth. Again, at five years old, I spent three months in the hospital. Again at 15 years old, I spent another three months in the hospital, not knowing if I would live or die. My father died when I was 19. As a young man in my early 20s, I was homeless on several occasions. I was addicted to marijuana, high for the majority of 12 years of my life. I was rejected by my church, misunderstood and wrongly accused by a friend I served, and in the process, I lost almost every friendship I had developed as a leader over 12 years of service, and there is still more. I understand brokenness and pain.

I don't share this for pity or to draw attention to myself. We all have stories wrought with pain. I share this because I can say with great confidence, my Jesus, my friend, brought me through every one of these scary, painful, and lonely seasons in His love. He has taken it all and used it to make me a better lover of God and people. We all suffer. What we do with it determines the fruit of our suffering. My prayer for myself and every reader is this: "Lord, take this pain and make us more like You through it." If we choose to surrender our pain as part of the process of forming Christ in us, we will walk in more compassion, patience, tolerance, grace, wisdom, kindness, hope, faith, and love. We *ARE* overcomers in Christ. Overcoming does not mean merely surviving; it means walking through the pain, doubt, and fear with the intention and commitment that through the process you are being formed to be just like Him. In this life, rejection, abandonment, false accusations, loss of loved ones and loneliness is unavoidable. They come in seasons, some short and others long. It is the broken condition of a world of sin. It is in these seasons we have the greatest opportunities for transformation. Every painful and difficult season is an opportunity to be transformed more into the image of Jesus — to love God and people more fully, more powerfully. The first step in overcoming the orphan and pauper spirits is being vulnerable to let God in and shine His light, revealing where you have agreed with lies.

The second step is being committed, at any cost, to the process of being transformed from a slave to a free child of God. We overcome these two spirits through the process of transformation. We cannot overcome through a grumbling, whining, or complaining spirit. That is like throwing gas on the fire. Grumbling, complaining, whining and the like is what orphans and paupers do. They are rooted in self-pity. Self-pity is a form of pride. It says, "Look at me; feel sorry for me. Give me your attention so I can feel better." That is pride. A traveling companion of self-pity is self-protection. Self-protection says, "No one really cares about me, so I have to protect myself and not allow anyone close. If I keep people distant, they won't hurt me, and I can stay hidden and safe." It sometimes comes in the form of self-comfort. Self-comfort says, "No one is there for me; no one really loves me. I will have to comfort myself because no one cares enough to comfort me." All these responses are prideful. They feed these spirits and build walls against God's love for you. Fear and pride go hand and hand. Fear says I am unlovable, and pride says I don't need anyone. Just like a toddler, we say internally, "by myself." The irony of it all is that we long for connection. Healthy, loving, transparent, vulnerable, and honest connection is the only kind that can fulfill our longing to be loved and belong.

If you have routinely struggled in this area, you need to be set free. In these cases, there is almost always a demonic stronghold influencing the way you process life—intellectually, emotionally, and relationally. If so, it is okay. I have been there, and I can tell you, you can get free. I am living proof of it. There is no reason to feel shame; to do so plays into the liar's hands. This has no, zero, zilch impact on your Father's love for you. If you feel otherwise, it is a lie—tell it to "shut up." You will be free. Draw close to Jesus, surrender to Holy Spirit, and be committed to the process. It is more than worth it.

Repenting and Renouncing

Repentance plays a powerful part in the process. In fact, freedom can't fully be realized until we repent from believing lies. When you were saved and repented from your sins, you were fully forgiven. The authority of the orphan and pauper spirits has been broken, along with the authority of everything else that is of the enemy. However, there is something called a stronghold. Strongholds can linger due to fear, pride, insecurity, anger, unresolved past hurts, and other lies we have agreed with. Removing them is a process. Inner healing ministry, when done with love and wisdom, is powerful to transform lives. Ministries like Sozo, Theophostics, Emanuel Prayer, and others of the kind can be very helpful to many and can help move things along. Having said that, you can walk through a good measure of the process—if not all of it—with just you, the Lord, and a few gifted and trustworthy friends.

The process of repentance and renouncing is incredibly important to the healing process. It might sound like work, and I guess in some ways and at some points there is a level of work involved in all growth. But remember, the Holy Spirit is with you through it all. Before I share with you how to apply repentance and renouncing, I want to be sure you have a solid understanding of strongholds.

What is a stronghold? Paul tells us in 2 Corinthians 10 what a stronghold is. His language tells us both how powerful a stronghold is, as well as the power we walk in as sons and daughters, once we fully take hold of our true identity. Paul states in verse 3, while we live in this world, we don't wage war as the world does. The world fights its wars through the force of controlling another. Whether war is done by reason, violence, physical conflict, or some other means, it is always about exerting control of one person's (or group of people's) will on others. Someone always loses their freedom to make choices for themselves. Even a victor who is benevolent exerts control and limits freedom to maintain order. The key word here is *control*. Paul is saying this is not the way God's children wage war. On the contrary, we have victory by doing the exact opposite. Our motives are not to control, but to deliver, to bring freedom and liberty to the captives.

Paul reveals Heaven's strategy. Our weapons are not carnal or worldly. Our weapons have divine power to demolish strongholds, fortresses and fortified places where the enemy has established protective walls to maintain control. The enemy sets up a place where he believes he has established an un-breachable position to maintain control. The Battle of Jericho is a good example. Scripture tells us Jericho was a "fortified" city. It means Jericho was a city built with defensive and strategic design for war. It was a fortress city, a stronghold. It was said no one had ever defeated Jericho's fortifications. The walls were so wide you could ride three chariots side by side. Armies were utterly defeated and broken on these walls. Paul is using this language when he speaks of the power we carry. Just as God brought down the walls of Jericho so devastatingly, we now walk in the same power for the deliverance of people.

Paul tells us what a stronghold is. He says in 2 Corinthians 10:5, *"We demolish arguments and every pretension that sets itself up against the knowledge of God..."* According to Paul, a stronghold, this mighty fortress we have the power to obliterate, is every vain philosophy, every tradition, every cultural belief, every value system, everything that stands against the truths of God -- who He is, who we are, His goodness, kindness, righteousness, His values, His wisdom, and His ways. These strongholds influence people, culture, media, entertainment, religion, politics, business, education, and of course family structures, even regions and countries. From the Fall on, Satan has built strongholds—ways of thinking, feeling, and believing—that influence people and society to keep God out of everything, while keeping his kingdoms of darkness in control.

In individuals, strongholds keep people in prison to their thoughts and emotions, thoughts rooted in fear.

This control keeps them from understanding and intimately connecting with God and His truth. The knowledge of God is not theological truth alone; it is knowing Him personally and allowing personal, experiential knowledge of Him lead us into intimacy. I always believed Jesus was the Son of God. I knew He was God. He was my Savior. My religion was built on these theological truths, but I did not know Jesus. He was far off, not near. When I came to the saving knowledge of Jesus, I didn't simply get better theology; I came to know and love a Person. I experienced Him, His love, and friendship. This revelation empowered me to more fully surrender to His Lordship. This was the beginning of tearing down strongholds.

The simplest and best explanation of a stronghold I have heard was shared by Vineyard pastor, Ed Piorek. In fact, from my understanding, he was one of the original Vineyard pastors from the 1970s. Ed came to Long Island around 1989 to do a conference called, "The Father's Love." The Holy Spirit had been talking to me for a while before this about the Father and His love, so I was very excited to hear more. In fact, I must give Ed and his teaching credit for launching me headlong into the pursuit of knowing the Father and knowing His great big love for me. In one of the sessions, he brought up strongholds as a point of bondage for many. I never really understood, or honestly even considered a stronghold. Ed said to picture a bird's nest. When you look at it, all you see are twigs, scraps of junk, and some mud packed in—a lot little of things that seem insignificant. "However," he asked, "have you ever tried to pull one apart? It is nearly impossible. Once formed, the careful weaving together of all the seemingly insignificant pieces with the mud is incredibly strong—it is a stronghold." From the time we were very, very young, the enemy has been sowing lies into our hearts and minds. Over time, all these little lies form a demonically empowered stronghold warring against knowing God. Lies like, "No one likes me. I don't fit anywhere. I am alone." Thoughts and emotions around rejection, death, health, family, love, and shame, pounding us again and again over the years, influencing and manipulating our experiences and perceptions of ourselves and others. Often, this is compounded by assuming things that aren't true. Other times, we magnify things to be more than they are. When our experiences are significantly traumatic, there can be a release of more power into the strongholds, causing us to bow to the influences of the enemy's lies in our lives, forming our self-view, our perception of others, and our experience of God's love for us personally.

How does this work? The enemy takes all these experiences and twists them over time to create a stronghold. This type of stronghold works like computer software. The stronghold determines how we process various experiences throughout our life. Relationships and circumstances are processed through these darkened thoughts and emotions, causing us to feel and respond in unhealthy ways. We begin to process relationships, our self-view, and our perceptions of God in such a way that keeps us from knowing the love of God. Every time certain situations come up, the software is activated and manipulates our perceptions. For many, this is the key reason they struggle to have a more stable walk with the Lord and with people. How powerful it is to be able to bring truth to destroy lies from the lives of those around us. I can tell you from my personal experience, when my strongholds began coming down, it was literally like the world was a brighter, more brilliant and vivid place to live. I began to think differently, and my whole perception of life influenced in the past by the strongholds shifted. I had greater clarity of truth, and in time, I learned to love and accept others more graciously. My view of who I was became healthier and healthier, and my compassion and love for others grew. It is truly amazing. After years of brokenness, strongholds of rejection, fear of man, fear of death, and abandonment came down. In their place, the Father's love brought acceptance, confidence in who I am as His son, life, and rest in Him. Whatever your stronghold is, the truth will be exactly the opposite. If it is rejection, the Father wants you to know you are fully accepted just the way you are; you don't need to work for His acceptance. If it is abandonment, He wants you to know He will never leave you. You will never be alone.

How do we tear down strongholds? We start with repentance. This may sound strange given that the enemy has done this to you. However, all freedom begins by taking responsibility. While we are victims, we are also complicit in that we've made choices to act and agree with lies. Remember, these are specific thoughts that have caused a personal paradigm, a pattern of thought and emotion that deny God's goodness and love. We need to repent for those thoughts and emotions, that come against or even judge His character. The Holy Spirit will show you these things. We cannot be free without taking responsibility for where we have agreed with the enemy.

Practically, how do we actively repent? Repentance literally means a 180-degree turn, a U-turn, if you will. We were thinking and living this way, we ask for forgiveness, and commit to go the opposite way. "Father, I believed in rejection. Because I have experienced rejection, I believed You would reject me, or have rejected me when things are not good in my life. Forgive me for believing a lie and allowing it to be a wall between us that has kept us from intimate connection. Help me believe the truth." That is what repentance looks like.

Renouncing is the second tool. Renouncing old patterns of thought is to stand in repentance, refusing to go back and believe the lies again. Every time the lying thoughts come up, you simply renounce them. You say, "No, I will not agree. This is a lie." Another way of saying it is, you reject those thoughts and abandon them, leaving them behind. This sounds easy enough, and sometimes it is. Other times, it is quite difficult because strongholds have a life to them. They have power, and they fight back in an attempt to reinforce the identity you have been held captive to. You need to be vigilant. If you slip up, simply repent, renounce, and move on. Do not allow yourself to entertain the questioning thoughts. Fixing your thoughts on the lies again will reinforce them, give them no place.

The way to freedom is a process. Sometimes it is instantaneous, most often it takes time. I had one stronghold that took over a year to obliterate. It took counseling, prayer, and a lot of renouncing. In my experience, there were times, I literally thought I was going insane. There was a spiritual battle I was going through for complete freedom. People I have ministered to often come back and tell me they feel like they are going crazy. I tell them that is good; keep doing what you are doing and keep getting counsel and prayer. They look at me like I am crazy, or ask, "Huh? How is that good?" My answer is always the same, and I have found this to be true in countless cases. If you weren't close to the victory, the enemy wouldn't be fighting so desperately. You are close. Press in, stay in the Word, worship intimately, keep getting prayer, keep rejecting the lies, rebuke the assailant, stay in community, and allow trusted friends and leaders to walk through the process with you. One of the worst things I have seen people do is isolate when they are in the battle. Isolation is exactly what the enemy wants. Stay connected with God and trusted friends. Be vulnerable and transparent, and let yourself be loved, first by the Lord and then by others. You are going to be amazed at what is about to happen. You will see everything with new eyes and a new heart. In every case, those that press through and don't quit come back and tell me, "You were right. It was amazing. Just when I thought I would lose it, I pressed in, broke down and wept deeply, and suddenly it felt like a thousand pounds came off me. And just like you said, I felt like everything was brighter and more beautiful. For the first time in my life, I feel free." This was my experience and the experiences of countless others I have helped walk through this. They did most of the work. I simply pointed them to Jesus and encouraged them not to quit. Holy Spirit is good at bringing us freedom.

You can be free. Trust God. Be honest with yourself and Jesus. Find a few trusted friends who will pray for you and keep you accountable in the process. Be sure they are encouragers. Commit to the process and be willing to do the work until you are free. You will get there, and it will be worth it. It is a beautiful thing to see yourself and others with His eyes.

The Supernatural Power of Generosity

I want to take a short moment to talk about generosity. Generosity in an unbeliever is an act of kindness. It is wonderful and demonstrates God is working through people, even those that do not know Him. However, extravagant generosity from a believer is powerful, especially in bringing down strongholds of materialism, fear of lack of provision, stinginess, greed, envy, etc. Generosity says, "I am going to give in fearless faith because I love You, Lord, and You are generous."

Tithes were taught in the Old Testament to instruct His people to give, so He could pour out blessings. In the New Testament, we have a new mandate. *"Give, and it will be given to you. They will pour into your lap a good measure — pressed down, shaken together, and running over. For by your standard of measure it will be measured to you in return,"* Luke

6:38. I have heard all types of arguments about how we don't need to tithe any longer, as if somehow giving to the mission of the church is an unfair burden. I have heard excuses about the way some televangelists and churches manipulate for money, how tithing has been misused by leaders, how all pastors should be tentmakers and feed themselves, forgetting the Scripture also says, *"Do not muzzle an ox while it is treading out the grain and the worker is worth his wages,"* 1Timothy 5:18. I was bi-vocational in ministry, as a youth pastor, worship pastor, associate pastor, church planter, and senior leader for 27 years. It was very difficult to effectively lead and work 40-50 hours a week. Most of those that take up this sentiment regarding tithing are still in bondage to an orphan and pauper spirit, or a religious spirit, and are playing along with it. They just don't want to give. If that's the case, just say so. The vast majority of leaders in the church serve with good and kind hearts. They give their lives and time away from family to care for others. Statistically, approximately 38% of churchgoers give regularly, and the majority that do, give less than 10%.

If we look at the scripture above in tandem with Malachi 3:10, we see that Jesus is not removing the tithes. He is removing the requirement of 10%. *"Bring the whole tithe into the storehouse, so that there may be food in My house, and test Me now in this,"* says the Lord of hosts, *"If I will not open for you the windows of heaven and pour out for you a blessing until it overflows."* Both scriptures say to test God with your giving and see if He doesn't abundantly bless. In Malachi, He will open the windows of Heaven and pour out overflowing blessings. In Luke, He says give and it will be given to you without measure. It will be so extravagant. If you have a fear of lack, be generous and test His faithfulness. Generosity is the stake you drive through the heart of a pauper spirit. Generosity is in the character of our Father, and if we are going to be like Him, generosity needs to be part of the character of His children. If this offends you, I would encourage you to take it to the Lord in prayer with a surrendered heart and be obedient to how He leads.

What people do with what we give to God through tithes and offerings is between them and the Lord. We have no control over what happens once we give. We aren't giving to a pastor; we are giving as worship towards Jesus. This is an act of praise and thanksgiving. Give it cheerfully as the Lord Himself has commanded. Once you have given, you have fulfilled your part, and you can position yourself for His blessing. What others do with it, don't worry about. The Lord is just and true. If someone is misusing funds, He will take care of it in His time. We just need to be faithfully obedient and protect our connection with the Father.

Chapter 7
The Father of Love, Light, and Life

*For this is the will of My Father, that everyone who looks
on the Son and believes in him should have eternal
life, and I will raise him up on the last day. John 6:40, ESV*

*At that day you will know that I am in My Father, and you
in Me, and I in you· He who has My commandments and
keeps them, it is he who loves Me. And he who loves Me will
be loved by My Father, and I will love him and manifest
Myself to him. John 14:20-21, NKJV*

*In that day you will ask in my name, and I do not say to you
that I will ask the Father on your behalf; for the Father
himself loves you, because you have loved me and have
believed that I came from God. John 16:26-27, ESV*

We have already talked a lot about Father God, but
He is worth a little more consideration. In John 14:6, Jesus
says, *"I am the way, the truth and the life."* John also says in
1 John 4:8 *"God is love,"* and in the Gospel of John chapter
one, the same Apostle says, *"God is light."* There is a
distinct correlation between Jesus' words in John's Gospel
and His words in 1 John. The way Jesus is pointing to is
the way of His love, loving like God. Without belaboring

what I have already said, God is perfect in love. He is love, and the way to life is through Him loving us, and our response to love Him and others with no strings attached. This is unconditional love.

The truth speaks of light. Light breaks through darkness. In John 1:5, he writes, *"The light shines in the darkness, and darkness did not overcome it."* Overcome or comprehend, as some versions translate, has to do with understanding. We can say *the truth revealed its light*, but dark hearts and minds couldn't understand it. The word truth in the Greek is *alithiea*. This word means several things, but ultimately it means "reality," what is real. When Jesus says, "I am the truth," He is saying "I AM your reality." His words are reality. They shift and impact everything. They will not return void because they are life. In the beginning, when the *logos*, the pre-incarnate Christ said, *"Let there be,"* he was shifting everything to release His reality, a superior and eternal reality. This understanding should shift many things for us—things like the authority to heal, deliver, and do miracles. Isn't faith the capacity to look at this world and trust in a greater reality? A reality where the person with cancer is healed. Heaven has invaded, and its reality is more powerful than this illusory one built on lies. When we understand who God is, we step into His truth, His reality, and our sonship. We position ourselves to step out in faith, bringing the reality of the Kingdom's rule and reign to earth. I fully understand we struggle with a world still at war with sin. This is the "now and not yet" of our experience. Some people are healed, while others are not. It is difficult to make sense of this. There is no perfect theological answer, but we need to understand the process of the Kingdom of God advancing. The Church does not need to be stuck in the "not yet" of unanswered prayers or use "not yet" as an excuse not to move forward into more. We are to live in the expectation of the "now." The "not yet" will be eradicated in due season. Our faithful call is to press into the now.

Jesus' core mission was to reveal the Father. He came to reveal, to bring light, and to make known what was not known before, what could not be comprehended.

"Listen carefully to what Jesus is saying: 'I came from the Father, while I am here I do only His will. Soon I will go back to My Father.' Jesus said my entire life was about the Heavenly Father. His coming to earth, His purpose while here, and His return. It was ALL about revealing the Father." David Wilkerson

This revealing of the Father is a reality-shifting revelation. Jesus' main purpose was to make the Creator of all things, the eternal Father, known. The intention of the Father was to make known the reality of His nature in ways we had never seen or understood before. When God makes Himself known in this type of dynamic way, by its very nature, it must shift our perception of reality. The miracles of Jesus testify to this truth. Suddenly, our understanding of the laws of nature are not quite adequate to explain what is happening. Today, people still stumble over this because they don't understand the superior reality of God's Kingdom released through faith. In John 15:1-5, Jesus begins His final teaching:

> *"I am the true vine, and my Father is the vinedresser. Every branch in me that does not bear fruit, He takes away; and every branch that bears fruit, He prunes it so that it may bear more fruit. You are already clean because of the word which I have spoken to you. Abide in me, and I in you. As the branch cannot bear fruit of itself unless it abides in the vine, so neither can you unless you abide in me. I am the vine, you are the branches; he who abides in me and I in him, he bears much fruit, for apart from me you can do nothing."*

He is the source of life; the Father is the one who loves Him, and through His love, we are connected to the Son *and* the Father. Everything flows from Him, through Jesus, to us. In the beginning, the Father said, "Son, say…" and the Spirit made it so. The reality shifted. Now, as we are connected with the Father in Christ, we get to enjoy a good measure of the reality of Heaven. Personally, I don't believe we have experienced as much of the Kingdom reality as is available to us. I know when Jesus comes, *"We will no longer see through a mirror dimly."* However, I wholeheartedly believe there is more available now — much more. One of the ways Jesus revealed the Father was through signs and wonders, healing, and the like. They revealed the Father's heart and the Kingdom reality — the truth of Heaven. They demonstrated His words were true and Heaven was invading; the Father was bringing the children home, taking back all that was lost, bringing things back to His intention.

As we rest in Him and receive His light, life, and love, we naturally bear fruit. The branches on the vine don't have to work to produce fruit. They simply receive from the vine, and the natural result is fruit. We rest and bear fruit. The fruit we bear is love, joy, peace, kindness, goodness, faithfulness, gentleness, and self-control. This is the natural fruit of God that comes from His character. As we abide, our character is transformed to be like His; we bear good fruit. We move in love.

Verse 2 reads, *"Every branch in me that does not bear fruit, He **takes away**; and every branch that bears fruit, He prunes it so that it may bear more fruit."* I want to take a few minutes to discuss this. Let me first say, I am not a Greek scholar. Having said that, I believe I am on very solid ground, and I am not alone in my thinking. It's my belief most translations are misapplying the Greek word interpreted "take away." This word in the Greek is aero. Aero means to lift up, pick up, or remove. Any one of those could be accurate. How do we determine which is most applicable? First, we look at the context of the verses. The first two branches are abiding vines. Abiding branches can only mean believers. The third are branches disconnected from the vine. They were either formerly connected or never were. No matter what, they are not connected now. This can only mean unbelievers, or those appearing to be believers, but were not actually connected. They will be cast aside and burnt. This can only mean unrepentant unbelievers. As scripture testifies, they will be cast in the fire. If a connected branch, a genuine believer, is not bearing fruit, removing it causes some theological issues. First, if works are not part of grace, why are they being removed because they aren't being fruitful? It would be contrary to our understanding of grace, not to mention the character of God. Second, it would mean being connected to Jesus is not enough, which would impact our view of the Cross. Neither of these are acceptable explanations. Therefore, there must be another application. When I was 19, I worked in a vineyard for a month in upstate New York. I worked there late April and early May. There were about 200 acres of grape vines for winemaking. The Finger Lake region in New York is known for its beauty and its wine. For four weeks, about ten young people did nothing but take bag ties and tie up grape vines to wires strung across posts. At the end of each season, the grapevines would be cut back to basically a stump. In late winter and early spring, the vines would grow rapidly on the ground. When they were two to three feet long, they would get "lifted up" off the ground to be closer to the sun, and so the flow from the roots could go up the vines branches and strengthen them. This way, they would all have fruit.

In ancient times, they didn't care for the vines and branches in this manner. The vines would grow on the ground. The weak branches were tied up to an arbor or trestle to allow them to receive more sunlight and be strengthened. Understanding John 15:2 in this light, "lifting up" the weaker branches, makes more sense in the context of these verses. The heart of God is to strengthen the weak in Him, not cut them off. This understanding affirms the character of God, and the truth of His grace. The heart of God is to take the weaker branches and draw them closer, so they might become healthy, strong, and bear fruit. He doesn't cut them off and discard them; that would not be love.

The Father is loving, kind, and tenderhearted. It doesn't mean He is a pushover. Love is not manipulative, nor does it allow itself to be manipulated. Honesty, integrity, and accountability are all a part of real love. However, this returns back to "those He loves He disciplines," so they can bear more fruit, walk in more love, and have more joy and peace. He is a good Father. He draws us near to Him, allowing His perfect love to cast out fear, transforming us in love.

A Prayer

Father God, thank You for the gift of Your beloved Son, Jesus, and for Your Spirit living in me. I pray for revelation, wisdom, and a tender heart to know You more fully. I desire to walk in intimacy with You, that Your Son, Jesus, and You, Holy Father, would be glorified in my life. Father, would You release the power of the Spirit of Adoption, Your Holy Spirit, to bring healing to all my father wounds and deliver me from every lie that steals Your love and my true identity as Your child? I forgive my earthy father for _____ and I repent for anything I have held against him. I release him to Your merciful hands and ask for Your mercy and kindness to abound to him. I also repent for every lie I have agreed with that is contrary to Your truth. I repent for my attitudes, opinions, traditions, and anything else that has blinded me to Your Love as my Father. From this moment forward, I commit myself to walking with You in wholehearted pursuit of Your heart and purposes for me. I am Your beloved child, and I desire to live from that reality. In the mighty and precious name of Jesus, Amen!

Chapter 8
The Spirit of Adoption

*For you did not receive the spirit of slavery to fall back into
fear, but you have received **the Spirit of adoption** as sons,
by whom we cry, "Abba! Father!"*
Romans 8:15, ESV (emphasis mine)

*For we know that the whole creation has been groaning
together in the pains of childbirth until now. And not only
the creation, but we ourselves, who have the firstfruits of the
Spirit, groan inwardly as **we wait eagerly for adoption
as sons,** the redemption of our bodies.*
Romans 8:22-23, ESV (emphasis mine)

The Spirit of Adoption is not some other spirit. It is
a title for Holy Spirit pointing to a specific role and
relationship for the believer. In order to fully understand
Romans 8, we have to first understand what adoption
meant to the readers of the letter. Paul was writing to
Jewish and Gentile believers in Rome. They were familiar
with Roman law. As a Roman citizen, Paul draws on his
knowledge of Roman law regarding adoption. In Rome,
one of the most common reasons for adoption was to
preserve an inheritance for a family who had no sons.
They would adopt a son from another family, and he

would receive all the rights and honors of a natural son. In fact, in some situations, he would receive more, because an adopted son could not be cast out later. He was a son for life. In addition, he had his inheritance from this point on. Under Roman law, the heirs didn't need to wait for the father to die to have an inheritance. The inheritance was shared by all regardless of age. However, the most interesting and perhaps significant reason was in Roman culture, every household needed a priest. Every Roman house was considered a place of worship. Not having a son meant there would be no priest in the household to lead worship. Their society depended on family worship. When Paul writes in Romans about receiving the Spirit of Adoption, and how all creation waits for the fulfillment of the adoption of the children of God, he is pointing to several things. First, we have been transferred from one family, one kingdom, to another. Second, this transference gives us a new father, God. By the Spirit, we can now call God *Abba*, which literally means Daddy or Papa. Third, we have access to our inheritance now. Finally, we are priests in His household. We have become a kingdom of priests.

The Holy Spirit, as the Spirit of Adoption, seals us as children of God. By His adoption, we cannot be kicked out, though we can choose to leave. We are made for worship, and we are free to receive Him. Worship is the open door to intimacy. As we worship, He draws us upward, close to Him, and our sonship is affirmed. Our worship also draws others into His presence. I have had many unbelievers come to the Lord simply by experiencing Him in worship.

Years ago, a young lady came to our church. She didn't know Jesus, she came with a friend, and I discovered she had been abandoned by her father when she was 12 or 13. As she got to know my family, she experienced love in ways she had not before. She had a very close relationship with her mom, and her stepdad was a good guy. However, when she spent time with us, she was seeing and experiencing a healthy, whole, functional family. She started coming to church from time to time. She "loved the music" and would say, "I feel so peaceful, but for some reason, I always cry." I told her "It's the presence of God. Jesus and the Father are loving on you." She told me, "It feels really good, like I am home." I didn't push anything, I just let the worship do the work. Eventually, she started listening to my sermons online. She came one day and said she wanted to give her life to Jesus and be baptized. The sons and daughters worshipping their Father made Him known to an orphan, and she fell in love with Him. This is what the Spirit of Adoption does.

I have been traveling the country since 2012, doing a conference that is now called "The Power of Sonship." We always have a time where we invite people to come forward and receive the Father's love in a fresh and powerful way. We focus particularly on those who question His love for them, though anyone can come up. We ask the Spirit of Adoption to come and pierce their hearts with arrows of the Father's love. It has been life changing for so many, as they have an encounter for the first time with the Spirit that is specifically and identifiably ministering His love as their Father. We have seen people sobbing and laughing, as well as demons leaving. It is powerful, and it is my passion to see every person come to know the Father in the fullness of His love — the love we have access to through Jesus Christ.

Grace Redefined

I could write a book on the subject of grace, and perhaps someday I will. For now, I want to share a little something on redefining grace. It is so important to have a full, biblical understanding of grace if we are going to live as sons and daughters. The Spirit of Adoption brings a revelation of grace that is so powerful, it is nuclear. It changes the very fiber of our being if we take hold of it.

The definition of grace universally held, taught, and quoted is, grace is God's "unmerited favor." I would propose grace is not simply God's unmerited favor, it is much more. In fact, I feel this definition comes up very short of what I have experienced in His grace.

I understand, when we look at being saved by grace, we don't deserve salvation; logic would then say we don't deserve grace. I understand that, and theologically, I wouldn't say it is wrong. This has been our understanding in the church for hundreds of years. However, grace is first and foremost a gift. Gifts are never merited. When a gift of love is shared between people, it is always free. If it isn't free, it is not a gift; it is a payment or a bribe. Grace is powerful. Grace is life, God-life.

When our attention in understanding grace is immediately drawn to "I don't deserve this," it causes us to focus on our brokenness. I want to recognize my brokenness; the point is, once we are "born again," merit is not relationally relevant any longer. Grace is now the flow of His life working in us as we abide in Him. Grace is an expression of His love and life, as well as His light, because grace reveals. Yes, before we come into Christ, grace is an unmerited gift we cannot earn. As I already said, no gift is earned. Some may say you are taking God's kindness for granted by thinking this way. I would strongly disagree. I exalt Him for His lovingkindness demonstrated by Him pouring out grace—His life and power—into and upon me. His grace is His provision for all we need. It is the power of God working in our life to love and live, transforming us into the image of His Son. What we lost in the Garden was the fullness of grace—the power and presence of His life for our sustenance in every area. Grace is an expression of His love, yes. But it is also the means to light and life.

I was wrestling with this question of grace a few years ago. I was speaking to my dear friend, David. David is a believing Jewish pastor and a very, very bright man. As I was fleshing out my thoughts, I shared how uncomfortable I was with the accepted definition of grace as unmerited favor. I shared how I believe for some, this narrow understanding has caused many to still identify themselves as sinners and not saints. I told him, in my mind and heart, it is so much more. It is empowering, transformative; it is provision for me to live out the gospel. David said, "Phill, do you know, in the Hebrew understanding, there actually is a grace that can, in a sense, be earned?" I was all ears. "Tell me, tell me!" He went on, "Yes, for us, there is a grace that would be something like this: When your son does something so wonderful, loving, and kind it compels you to run to him, hug, and kiss him. What he did moved your heart towards him, compelling love in action, your embrace." I was blown away. Yes, Yes, Yes—of course there must be actions that move the heart of God in love and joy, releasing a grace that is relational, flowing from a proud Father. It is not about loving one more than others. It is about relationship. If we can't move His heart, what type of relationship would it be? Every good father's heart is moved when he sees his children loving the way he has taught and modeled love. Isn't it amazing? We can move our Father's heart by the way we love Him and others. Our love and unselfish service, our extravagant generosity through perseverance in faith and hope is so beautiful to Him. He draws near and releases a new measure of grace and intimacy.

Yes, grace is a gift—the perfect gift of love. Grace empowers us to do what we cannot do on our own. Grace gives us life—His life. We can position ourselves for increased life in Him by the way we love Him and others. Grace is beautiful, powerful, and transforming; it is His love and life working in our hearts and lives, transforming our hearts to be like His, making Him known through our life.

All mankind has a measure of God's grace; without it, we couldn't live. However, when a person receives the saving grace of God — the unearned, unmerited, empowering gift — they say, "Yes, I give You my life. I receive the amazing grace released at the Cross. I surrender my life to You alone, Jesus. I am born again, a new creation, Your son." When the Spirit of God comes and inhabits us, we enter a whole new greater measure of grace. The Holy Spirit, the Spirit of Adoption, comes and indwells us, and this new, greater grace begins to reveal Jesus more fully; the ultimate truth of the Father comes alive in us. We begin to experience the Father's love. As we embrace the truth, surrendering ourselves and leaving our old self behind, the Spirit of Adoption brings greater and greater revelation and experience of the Father's love. This transforms our hearts. As we embrace the process of transformation, our hearts begin to be fashioned to function with His love.

The Metamorphosis of our Soul

In Romans 12, Paul speaks of a metamorphosis we all are going through. This process is dependent on our willingness to truly surrender control. It is scary to release control. It stirs up our worst trust issues. However, real relationship requires a release of control and a choice to trust. It is the same in our walk with the Lord. To know Him more fully, we need to be willing to be more fully known. That is what intimacy is built upon — two parties willingly surrendering control to the other, willing to make their hearts known and shared, risking trusting the other. This can be difficult and painful. Most of us carry significant relational hurt where our needs were unmet, and our feelings were not affirmed, in relationships we thought we could trust. Strongholds tells us to stay closed, don't risk, protect yourselves, because no one else will. These positions kill relational intimacy. If we want a love that is real, deep, and lasting, risk is required. In fact, we were made for these types of relationships. We need them to be whole. We need to both receive and give to these types of relationships. It is why we were made. For this transformation to occur, we need to die to ourselves. To be a new creation, the old must be gone, dead. Dead men don't hold grudges. They don't care what people think about them. They don't protect themselves. They aren't quick to anger; they are dead. Dead men don't have a fear of man, they don't need man's approval, and they don't judge; they are dead. Do you get the point? We only care about these things—to quote The Princess Bride—because we are only "mostly dead," not fully dead. This is the process—dying to self, so we can come fully alive in Christ. The sooner the better. All the treasures of Heaven are on the other side. Our inheritance is on the other side. When we die to self, we get the fullness of Jesus and the love the Father has for Him.

How do we do this? How do we die to self? This is the million question, isn't it? I remember when I first realized the cost of gaining Him fully, I was scared. The cost seemed overwhelming, though I didn't really know what it was I was so afraid of. One night after our Home Group, I had released everyone, but I asked my wife and one trusted friend if they would pray with me after everyone left. I knew this was going to be big and didn't want to be seen a blubbering mess in front of the entire group. As they started to pray for me, I began to weep, quietly and slowly. With tears running down my cheeks, moving towards my neck, I shared, "The Lord is pressing into some deep places of hurt in me, but even more so, things I need to let go of to change." As I was sharing this with them, I got a picture of a very fat long root, with hundreds of feeder roots of different lengths. It looked like a carrot, but much bigger; it was huge. I heard the Lord say to me, "You have this great big root in you. It goes deep. This root is the key; it is what keeps My love out. I am going to take this root out." I responded, "Yes Lord, rip it out whole. I just want to be free. I can't take this much more, and I want You." The Father spoke back to me, "No, if I were to take it all in an instant, the pain would overwhelm you and the hole it would leave in your heart would be devastating to you. I am going to cut off the feeder roots. As I cut them, the large root will begin to die. When it is fully dead, I will pull it out. What will be left is a perfect hole just right for Me to place the seed of My love. It will grow and blossom, and all the fear will be gone." I knew it was an amazing gift. I was also still terrified. I shared this with Patti and our friend Denise. Denise asked me, "What are you afraid of? It is an amazing picture." Perhaps some of you can relate to the big fear I had. I answered, "As much as I don't like this version of me, it is the only me I know. What will I be if I let go completely? I don't know what I will become or what the cost will be." As much as we want God's love, we often struggle with letting go of the familiar, letting go of control. I didn't like me, but I knew this me. I knew the secrets, pain, and hurt I held on to. I had accepted this broken version of me and knew how to protect him. What would I become? Would I really know God more fully, and would He really love me? These are real fears. They are lies, but the feelings are very real. They represent the old person. The old person must die if the new creation is going to be fully realized this side of Heaven. This is the way to freedom. Even as He died for us, we are called to die for Him. It is the transformation from death to life we are promised.

*Do not be conformed to this world, but **be transformed** by the renewal of your mind, that by testing you may discern what is the will of God, what is good and acceptable and perfect. Romans 12:2, ESV (emphasis mine)*

This one verse speaks volumes if we understand what Paul is teaching. First, there is a play on words with 'conform' and 'transform.' To conform means to fashion yourself as another. It means to make yourself like another form. Let me give an example. We were all young once and have done this or have seen others do it. You just started in middle school or high school. There are people you just met. They seem like they are popular, and you want to fit in. In fact, fitting in is a high priority amongst teens. You notice they all dress a certain way or have certain expressions or activities. You have little interest in any of that, but you want to fit in and be accepted. You want friendship and you want to have fun. So, after a few days, weeks, months, you are dressing like them, talking like them and doing the things they do. That is conformity. Conformity comes in all different ways. It is easy to see the things in the world we don't want to conform to. The pressure not to conform is often hard for a new believer. It could cost relationships, the difficulty of giving up unhealthy things and it even can cause turmoil in families. But, to conform in this context is to maintain something that is false and rooted in fear. Conformity kills our unique individuality.

This can also happen in the Church. Religion is all about conforming. In fact, religion demands conformity since the goal of religious groups is to have everyone behave the same, agree on the same things and conform to fit in, avoiding any messes caused by someone being different.

I have been in ministry in the Association of Vineyard Churches since 1988. We had a slogan then, and many Vineyard churches still use it; it is a good slogan. "Come as you are." Our meaning is, come with your mess. Come and belong and be loved. The Vineyard was originally launched out of Calvary Chapel in southern California. Back in those days, Hawaiian shirts were in vogue in southern California. You know the shirts — flowers or palm trees all around, straight bottom to be worn out of your pants. It became a joke that all Vineyard pastors wore Hawaiian shirts. It was almost true, but not quite. Now, I remember someone coming to church in a suit. He came in suits every week for probably three weeks. His children also came very dressed up, as did his wife. One day, they came in business casual. I asked, "Hey, what happened to wearing your suits?" He said, "No one else here wears them, so it felt weird wearing them. It felt like we didn't fit." I asked him, "Do you like wearing suits?" "No, not really, but in my last church, everybody did. It seemed like that was expected." I told him, "It's okay if you don't like wearing suits, but if you do, wearing them is okay here too. We aren't going to keep you at a distance. Come as you are means whatever is comfortable for you. Whoever you are, you are acceptable." You see, if he changed his dress style, not because he preferred not to wear a suit, but to fit in, that would be conformity, making yourself to fit another's pattern. This happens in every area of society, including the Church. Conformity is about changing your externals in order to belong. A key problem arises from this mentality, particularly in the Church; people hide their true self for fear of rejection, judgment, and abandonment. We hide our deep pain, our secret sin, staying in bondage. Then, when people fall, especially leaders, we wonder how it was possible. Conformity — everyone speaking and acting the same way — has made an unsafe place for real intimacy and wholeness.

Where conformity is all about the externals, transformation can only happen from the inside out. I find it fascinating Paul uses the word "transformation" when addressing this process. The Greek word for transformation is *metamorphóō*. It is where we get the word metamorphosis. Years ago, I was studying Romans 12:2. I love to look up the original Greek for certain key words in a verse. I am not a Greek scholar, but I do have a Ph.D. in Google. I also love to find biblical themes that can be seen in nature. You know, "The natural things speak of the invisible." So, as any good Doctorate of Google would do, I began the search. The obvious place I started was looking up metamorphosis—what does it look like? Ah, of course caterpillars and butterflies. I took science in school, as we all have, and I thought I understood metamorphosis. A caterpillar makes a cocoon. It stays in the cocoon and a chemical reaction happens. Somehow, the caterpillar gets wings, and now it is a butterfly.

My general understanding was minimally correct. The caterpillar has an internal clock telling it when its life is ending, so it has time to make a cocoon. When the cocoon is made, the caterpillar dies. It isn't until the caterpillar dies that the process begins. Once dead, a chemical reaction starts. Everything the caterpillar once was breaks down until there is nothing left but a gooey chemical-filled liquid. This is the exciting part. I love this part. Hidden in the caterpillar for all those weeks are these dormant cells called "imaginal cells." The caterpillar's immune system keeps attacking them, but they keep multiplying faster and faster, until the caterpillar's immune system can't keep up, and eventually gives up. This is how the caterpillar passes on. In the right season, the imaginal cells come alive and take over the earthy creature until nothing is left.

The imaginal cells come together in clumps or groupings. They all start to resonate with the same frequency and start sharing information. After a while, as they are resonating all to the same frequency, the clumps start coming together into larger clusters. They keep clustering until there is a long line of clustered groups. The groupings form a larger bond as they all resonate in one accord. At this stage, they are passing information one to another. This little community of "imaginal cells," are all sharing information in the chrysalis. At some point, as they have been sharing information, connecting and communicating, an amazing thing happens. These clusters of imaginal cells form one strand of separate cells. They start to communicate the order of things. We are an eye. Us, too! We are the heart. Awesome! Hey, we are a wing. Us, too! And so on. Each cluster of cells fits into the place they were made for, with all the others cooperating so they function perfectly as a whole. Pretty amazing, right?

A creature that could only crawl in the dirt and see life from below dies so a more beautiful creature can come to life—a creature designed and empowered for flight, who sees life from a heavenly perspective. One devours leaves, the other drinks nectar from flowers. They couldn't be more different. One dies so another can be formed.

The beauty of God's creation in the natural points to the beauty of the eternal. Just like the caterpillar has cells carrying the DNA for something greater and more beautiful, every human soul carries imaginal cells longing to bring them into a transformed state. New-Agers are searching for the key to ascendance, having bought into a belief system that says we are all collectively god; if we do this or that enough, we can transcend this world to a higher level of awareness. What they don't understand is Christ, grace, and a good Father. They don't understand He is a personal God who created man for intimate relationship. They strive for what every believer has. They strive from pride and the desire to hold on to their own life and ways. None the less, they are also His children. Jesus loves them. We are to reveal the better way, the only way. The true Way is through the Cross, and the Cross leads to death. But we have the resurrection.

We were buried therefore with him by baptism into death, in order that, just as Christ was raised from the dead by the glory of the Father, we too might walk in newness of life.
Romans 6:4, ESV

Notice the tense of this verse. It is past tense, "we were buried." When we are born again and baptized, there is a supernatural event taking place. *Our old self dies on the Cross with Jesus.* You are dead, or at least mostly dead, though it often doesn't feel like it in your experience. This is the process of transformation. The caterpillar makes the cocoon but doesn't die right away. For all intents and purpose, he is dead when the cocoon is done. However, his immune system goes on fighting off the imaginal cells until they cannot be stopped. The old self fights off the new, until the new overwhelms it. This exactly describes the process we are in. When Paul says do not conform but be transformed, this is what he is pointing to. I don't know about you, but I would do anything to soar above the things of the earth. I mean, wouldn't you? In every person, there are spiritual imaginal cells waiting for us to come to the Cross and die so we can be transformed into the image of our Father, the Maker of all things. There is something in us that hungers for more. We seem to innately know there is something higher, healthier, and more beautiful than what we have here.

Paul moves on to tell us when we are transformed, we will be able to know, discern, and understand God's will. The will of a person is in the heart. Paul is saying we will know His heart. When we know and have His heart, we will walk in the perfection of His love and in the power of His Spirit. Figuratively speaking, your God-created, spiritual imaginal cells are awakened! Let go and let them grow. They carry your Heavenly Father's spiritual DNA. They carry the capacity for you to be formed into the image of His Son.

Another amazing thing is how all the imaginal cells resonate to the same frequency drawing them together, recognizing each cluster's role, and making room for each cell to step into what God made them for.

When we, believers, resonate with the frequency of God—His love, light, and life—we make room for other people's gifts, realizing we are more with them than we are without them. When this happens, we together soar like eagles.

The Spirit of Adoption, Holy Spirit, is working all these things in us, making us into the image of our Father. Soon the world will know we are His by the way we love each other. We will love one another exactly as our Father and precious Savior Jesus love each other and love us.

Chapter 9
The Father's Love Redefines Us

How great is the love the Father has lavished on us that we should be called children of God! 1 John 3:1, NIV

Praise be to the God and Father of our Lord Jesus Christ, who has blessed us in the heavenly realms with every spiritual blessing in Christ. For he chose us…. In love he predestined us to be adopted as his children. Ephesians 1:3-5, NIV

*I will make my dwelling among them and walk among them, and I will be their God, and they shall be my people· Therefore go out from their midst, and be separate from them, says the Lord, and touch no unclean thing; then I will welcome you, and **I will be a father to you, and you shall be sons and daughters to me**, says the Lord Almighty. 2 Corinthians 6:16-18, ESV (emphasis mine)*

My sincere hope in writing this book is that you would be empowered to take hold of the Father's love for yourself. Coming to know Him as Abba, Papa, Father God has radically changed my entire life.

When Jesus was ready to launch out in ministry, He had a powerful experience. The event I am going to

147

share is what drove Him and empowered Him to go from the wilderness all the way to the Cross. In Matthew 3:16-17, we have the story of Jesus' baptism. Jesus has come to John the Baptist to be baptized. *"Let it be so now, for thus it is fitting for us to fulfill all righteousness," Matthew 3:15.* Jesus is committed to being fully man, and therefore, righteousness would require baptism. John accepts His request, and when Jesus comes up from the water, a remarkable thing occurs. If we have read the Bible more than once, or ever attended a Good Friday or Easter Sunday service, we have surely heard this story. In verse 16 it reads, *"And when Jesus was baptized, immediately he went up from the water, and behold, the heavens were opened to him and he saw the Spirit of God descending like a dove and coming to rest on him And a voice from heaven said, "**This is my Son, whom I love; with him I am well pleased**" (Matthew 3:16).*

Jesus hadn't done a single thing in ministry. Not a single sermon or healing. The Father wanted to affirm Jesus' sonship before the launch of his ministry. His ability to start and finish the mission was rooted in this reality: His Father loved Him and was pleased with Him. He went into the desert fully submitted and willing to pay the price, whatever the cost. The Father was securing in His son the knowledge of Whose He was, His right identity. The Son belonged to His Father, and His Father adored Him. What was the enemy's first assault on Jesus in the wilderness? *"If you are God's Son..."* He attacked Jesus' identity in the Father. The Father's blessing, affirming the sonship of Jesus, empowered Jesus to defy the devil.

It is the revelation of the Father's passion for the Son that drives Jesus from this day onward. Likewise, my Father loves me with all He is; I am going to respond in love. I will be obedient to the end. As my sons were growing up, I told them, "Obedience is one way we say I love you." Obeying the Lord is one way we demonstrate worship and love.

When the Father blesses Jesus with those words, He is saying to every one of us, "I love you for who you are, My sons and daughters. There is nothing you can do that could possibly make Me love you more than I did the day you were born. I will love you extravagantly, not just for your life on earth, but for all eternity, My heart will be filled with love and passion for you. Receive My love, and know I am with you always, through every painful circumstance. My love will bring beauty from ashes and joy from sorrow. I will bring life in every way."

When John tells us in 1 John 3:1, "How great is the love the Father has lavished on us that we should be called children of God!" he is speaking in poetic language, telling us how God romances us with extravagant love. In essence, we are being told "the God Who is love" is extravagantly pouring Himself out in our lives. A good picture of this is in the synoptic Gospels: Matthew, Mark, and Luke. Jesus is reclining at the table with the twelve disciples, Lazarus, and probably others. Mary comes in and lavishly pours out very expensive oils on Jesus' feet. The oils may have been worth a year's wages. I don't know if that is accurate, but what is clear is, they were worth a lot of money — to the point the disciples themselves considered it a waste. She took this very, very expensive oil and poured it out on Him lavishly. Picture the woman coming with an alabaster jar, maybe 24 ounces, and just pours it out on your feet. This is how the Father loves ALL His beloved children. That includes you, right where you are, with all your stuff. Right now, without measure, He is pouring out His love — Himself.

The Father's Love Redefines Humility

False humility is when we act in a way that appears humble for man's approval. False humility is a form of pride. It says, "Look at me — I am good." It is an expression of shame. A person who struggles with false humility cries out, "Look at me! I am good." However, when there is nothing to gain, the true driving force — pride — will stick its head up. These people can be braggards, puffed up, and manipulative. False humility is always self-seeking. What is true humility? Humility is self-awareness in the best, most healthy way. It accepts both our strengths and weaknesses. It is not driven by the need for approval. It sees integrity and authenticity as a higher value than friendships built on lies. Someone that embodies true humility is not threatened by other peoples' giftings. They know their gifts, have confidence in where they are strong, and therefore, can encourage and build up those around them. At no point does the scripture show, evenly remotely, that Jesus ever denied who He was. He was the most humble man who ever lived. He knew who He was, and that was enough for Him. He didn't need to be someone else. He liked exactly who He was.

We should never be afraid of offending people because we simply know who we are. The religious leaders often accused Jesus of arrogance when He was speaking His true identity as God's Son. I love this Bill Johnson quote: "Confidence looks like arrogance to the insecure." Isn't that true? The insecure will always be threatened by those who have confidence in who they are. The shame residing in insecure people will be offended by those who walk in the assuredness of who they are. It makes them uncomfortable. For us, the key is to love them well, encouraging them in who they are, until they learn to love and like themselves.

Love is Redefined for us in Two Ways

Whoever confesses that Jesus is the Son of God, God abides in him, and he in God· So we have come to know and to believe the love that God has for us. God is love, and whoever abides in love abides in God, and God abides in him. By this is love perfected with us, so that we may have confidence for the day of judgment, because as he is so also are we in this world. 1 John 4:15-17, ESV

Love is redefined for us by the Holy Spirit in two ways: externally and internally. The scripture above speaks about how the Spirit does this. John repeats the teaching of Jesus in John 15; the key is abiding. Abiding means to rest, remain, stay close. It speaks of relationship between two people, where something is shared and gained by both, in and through the bond. For instance, in John 15, when Jesus says, "Abide in Me and I will abide in you," He is speaking of staying relationally connected. In the scripture above, John is reminding the readers God is love, and when we abide in Him, we abide in love. When we rest in Him, stay connected, stay close to, and wait on Him, we are in a love bond that transforms us. It is in abiding in fellowship with the Lord that we gain the confidence that we are His. Out of this confidence flows the life and power of God for us, and out through us to others.

Internally

Whoever confesses and acknowledges that Jesus is the Son of God, God abides in him, and he in God. We have come to know, [by personal observation and experience] and have believed [with deep, consistent faith] the love which God has for us. God is love, and the one who abides in love abides in God, and God abides continually in him. In this, [union and fellowship with Him] love is completed and perfected with us, so that we may have confidence in the day of judgment [with assurance and boldness to face Him]; because as He is, so are we in this world. 1 John 4:15-17, Amplified Bible (emphasis mine)

Again, abiding. Abiding is difficult for many. How do we have relationship and not do something? It doesn't come naturally to us to simply embrace a relationship we don't have to do something for. We enter a relationship expecting we need to do something to hold on to it. We think abiding means we simply do nothing. That is not the case; there is a lot we need to do to abide. The scripture doesn't say to simply abide. John focuses in on the kind of abiding we are to press into. We are to "abide in His love." We are to rest in His love. We are to take it into our souls. We are to affirm His love for us when fear rises. When we can say no to fear, which is what renouncing is, and affirm His love for us, we return to abiding. Another way to say abide in My love is to say live inside His love. This is an internal state that brings transformation.

How do we do this practically? How do we impact our soul in a way that brings His love into our experience more fully?

As strongholds come down, we must fill those places with His love. In Matthew 12:43, Jesus says, *"Now when the unclean spirit has gone out of a man, it roams through waterless places in **search of rest**, but it does not find it. Then it says, 'I will return to my house from which I came.' And when it arrives, it finds the place unoccupied, swept, and put in order."* While Jesus is specifically speaking of deliverance, the same reality can occur with strongholds. Notice in verse 43, it tells us demons look for a place to rest — a place to abide. Strongholds are places the demonic has built in order to control, exert power and authority, causing destruction in and through the victim. Strongholds are torn down through repentance and renouncing, simply saying no, "resist(ing) the devil and he will flee." When strongholds come down, we need to fill our souls with His love and build a stronghold of truth. We want our thoughts and emotions to line up with His truth. This is where the work of abiding is worked out. It is not working for approval. It is working from approval. It is resting in the truth that empowers us to abide in the reality of His love.

We do this with several tools that are powerful weapons. First, worship. Cultivate a devotional worship life, not one out of religious disciplines. If it is nothing more than a discipline, it will lead to relational death. It is walked out in a romance—not a flighty romance, but one that is filled with passion, devotion, and awe. When I was falling in love with my wife, I loved to hear her voice, especially her laugh. We would talk on the phone for an hour or more at a time. We talked about everything going on in her life and mine, but mostly hers. Not because she was self-centered, but because I loved to hear about her. It was me romancing her. If I could get her to laugh, even better. This is one of the wonderful and powerful ways Jesus wants us to relate to Him. He wants to romance us; He enjoys it when we romance Him. This will look a little different for each person, but the same relational keys are relevant to us all. Worship is powerful in building intimacy. If we understand what worship really is, we can't help but engage Him in it. God doesn't call us to worship Him because He needs our constant affirmation. He isn't insecure and in need of us to tell Him He is wonderful. In worship, we lift our hearts, our very soul, to Him. As we lift our hearts to Him, He comes and takes us to Himself. As we live in this heart-to-heart connection with the One who loves us perfectly, we reach out to those around us, drawing them to do the same. As we reach out with our hearts in surrender, we open up to the Lord. As we open to Him, He comes and fills us with His love. He calls us to worship because it is the place we become one with Him in the most intimate way. In this place, He gets to enjoy all we are, and we get to enjoy all He is. Worship shifts everything. As we engage, He comes and shifts the atmosphere around us and even our heart.

Speaking in tongues is also incredibly powerful. There are two kinds of tongues. One is corporate tongues. This is the functioning of this gift in corporate worship. The Holy Spirit moves our spirit to declare through our voice the greatness of God. This is a powerful expression of the gift. However, the other expression of this gift, our personal, spirit-led prayer language, is powerful to shift things and draw us upward. It is a gift that comes with the Holy Spirit. The Holy Spirit engages our spirit to speak prayers and words that shift darkness and bring us upward to Him. When I am feeling like the spiritual atmosphere is overcoming intimacy and I don't know what to pray, or perhaps don't care to, I will pray in tongues until everything shifts and I feel His presence. If you do not have your prayer language, don't worry. All the gifts are "of the Spirit." If you have been baptized in the Holy Spirit, you have all the gifts residing in you because the Holy Spirit is in you. Simply ask the Lord to activate this gift, and if need be, ask someone you trust that has the gift to pray with you for it.

The Word of God is non-negotiable in every believer's life. If you are a child of God, a disciple of Jesus, you must be in the Word of God. Hebrews 4:12 says, *"For the word of God is living and active, sharper than any two-edged sword, piercing to the division of soul and of spirit, of joints and of marrow, and discerning the thoughts and intentions of the heart."* The Word of God truly is alive. Jesus is the Logos. In Greek, "logos" means "word," or "the message." In John 1, it says the Logos was with God, and the Logos was God. Jesus is the Word in the flesh. The entirety of Scripture testifies of who He is and what He values. Being in His Word is like eating truth and digesting it in your soul. I have had countless people tell me, "I don't like to read." Today, you don't even need to read; you can get the Bible on audio. However, there is something powerful about reading the Word, especially when you read it out loud. When you have both the hearing and seeing senses engaged, there seems to be a powerful effect. Some say, "When I read the Bible, I don't understand what I am reading." That is fine. You should join a Bible study because you need to know the Word. I have also heard, "I like listening to so-and-so. I like the way they teach. I get the Word from them." My answer is, "If you don't know it for yourself, how will you know if what they are teaching is accurate, biblical truth?" Be Berean; know the Word of God for yourself. Meditating on God's Word is another practical and relational discipline that is very valuable. Meditating on His Word is when we take a verse, sit quietly and contemplatively, chew on it, and ask the Holy Spirit to reveal His truth in it. Those that speak against Christians meditating are wrongly addressing the topic from a place of fear and misunderstanding. They confuse it with transcendental meditation. In transcendental meditation, you empty yourself and transcend your sense of self. This, you should not do. It opens us to the demonic. In Hebrew, the word meditate, *hagah*, means to "ponder, contemplate, muse, consider, or chew on." It is an exercise in drawing near to the Lord in rest. I have a good friend, Tad Blackburn, who is a brilliant pastor, leader, and counselor. While he has a Ph.D. in counseling, he has a deeper place, God's heart. He once said, "Peace is resting in God's love, and joy is dancing in God's love." I love that, it's beautiful. Meditating on His Word is a tool that brings us into His Sabbath rest. We were created for intimacy with the Lord, the byproduct of which is peace and joy. As we quietly meditate, contemplate, and ponder scripture with the Holy Spirit, we find life and peace from and in Him. It is a powerful weapon, and it is invaluable in learning how to walk in rest in the midst of a busy world. If you would like to learn more on how to do this, I recommend my friend Charles Bello's book, "*Prayer As A Place.*"

There are many other ways to connect and abide in Him and His great love. My wife loves to go on walks and sees Him in nature. She connects with Him by pondering what He has made. My brother is an artist, and he connects intimately with Jesus as He paints or draws. I know quite a few artistic people who connect in much the same way. I like to get my guitar out and sing my prayers to Him with authenticity, vulnerability, and complete honesty, based on what is going on in me. I know many others who do the same. This is one of my favorite love languages with Jesus and Abba.

You may have some other way to connect. Whatever brings you into His presence and helps you rest in the knowledge of His great love, whatever brings you to His arms of love and is noble, pure, and true, go for it. Whatever works for you, commit it to Jesus, make yourself available to Him, and do it consistently. Just as it is in any intimate relationship, when communication goes down, intimate, meaningful, life-giving connection goes with it.

Consider this: God is love; God is in me, and I am in Him. Therefore, I carry in me perfect love. I am a love carrier. Therefore, I am empowered and anointed to love all those around me. The only thing in the way is fear.

Externally

> *Beloved, let us love and seek the best for one another, for love is from God; and everyone who loves is born of God and knows God. The one who does not love has not become acquainted with God, for God is love· By this the love of God was displayed in us, in that God has sent His only begotten Son into the world so that we might live through Him. I John 4:7-9, Amplified Bible*

Living love is part of the continuous revelation of who God is. John is sharing a revelation of God's love that

158

is made evident by how we love others. John isn't just speaking about love. He is talking about a love working out through how we honor others. This scripture gives us a wonderful understanding of "honor." Authentic love always honors. When we love others with wholehearted commitment to seek what is for their best, without concern for ourselves, that is honor. Honor is what love looks like in community. When we live out our relationships in this way, we have drawn close to the Lord. Love attracts love, and love must multiply. When we love with His love, Abba draws close and the fruit is a greater capacity to love. For us to be able to love more generously, for our love to expand, we need a greater revelation of His love. It is the cycle of love that transforms us into maturity in Christ. As God loves us and we receive His love, we are empowered to love others. As we love others, they have a revelation of God. They receive His love and go and love others. On the other side, as we love them, God comes and gives us more love. Our love tank only empties when we shut the Lord out, or we stop actively loving others. We were made from love, for love, to love, through love; He is all about love. Additionally, love with honor brings life. The only commandment with a promise, "Honor your mother and father so that you would have long life . . . " Honor brings life to our relationships, overflowing to those around us.

Loving Yourself to Love Others

Wherever I go to speak, I often ask this question: "Are you a sinner or a saint?" I am always amazed, and it breaks my heart to see the number of God's children who identify themselves as sinners. I would estimate, from all the times I have done this, it has been no less than forty percent, and in many cases, closer to seventy percent. Why? The failure must fall on those who lead.

Romans 6:5-11 unwraps the truth regarding sin. Pay close attention to what Paul says in these verses. They are the key for understanding who you are, sinner or saint.

> *For if we have been united with him in a death like his, we shall certainly be united with him in a resurrection like his. We know that our old self was crucified with him in order that the body of sin might be brought to nothing, so that we would no longer be enslaved to sin. For one who has died has been set free from sin. Now if we have died with Christ, we believe that we will also live with him. We know that Christ, being raised from the dead, will never die again; death no longer has dominion over him. For the death he died he died to sin, once for all, but the life he lives he lives to God. So you also must consider yourselves dead to sin and alive to God in Christ Jesus.*

Paul is shedding light on a supernatural truth. We have been crucified with, or in Christ. Our old self, our self before we received Holy Spirit, was crucified with Christs—past tense—when we received Christ in our

160

hearts and were cleansed by His blood. When Christ took on all the sin of all the people who have ever lived or will ever live, He took our sin with Him to the Cross. He did this, so we would be completely set free from the influence of sin.

Paul says, *"Now if we have died with Christ, we believe that we will also live with Him."* Those of us that gave our hearts to Jesus, trusting He paid for all our sin — not just the sin up to the time we were baptized, but every sin from cradle to the grave — are dead, in terms of our old self. We are now "alive in Him." You are already alive in Christ, a *new creation.*

Paul wraps this up with the most profound statement. *"For the death he died he died to sin, once for all, but the life he lives he lives to God. So you also must consider yourselves dead to sin and alive to God in Christ Jesus."* The death Jesus died, He died to sin. He doesn't say for sin, but "to" sin. What does that mean? He died to completely release us from bondage "to" sin. He did this once for every single human being that has lived, is living, or ever will live. When Jesus died on the Cross, He went right into Hell, kicked sin squarely in the teeth and said, "You are now powerless against Me and My children." He snatched the keys of Hades and said, "You're not locking up any that are Mine ever again." When all that was done, He resurrected, completing the mission. The life Jesus now lives is to God, not in His divinity, but in His humanity.

Paul drives this home for us. *"So, you also must consider yourselves dead to sin and alive to God in Christ*

Jesus." This word 'consider' in the Greek, *logozomai*, also means to reckon or conclude. "Reckon" is an accounting term, i.e. our books have been reckoned, meaning the books are balanced. Everything is as it should be. The adjustments to balance it all and come to a good, final reckoning are done. We must take hold of the truth that our debt is fully paid—past, present, and future; it is done!

So, why do we sometimes sin? That is the question we all stumble on. Our redeemed spirit does not sin. Our soul can sin, but that doesn't make us a sinner. How does that work? It comes from us doubting that our sin is dead in Christ. The enemy and our flesh manipulate us to act in a way that is contrary to who we are, the fully redeemed children of God. When we doubt who we are, we open the door to old sin actions. We are familiar with these false comforters. We start to smell, feel, and hear the things that drew us towards sin. We feel shame or fear, and we give in. Then shame takes over, and we say, "I am a worthless sinner." That is the lie. You are a saint of God. What is a saint? Catholicism has dramatically influenced our understanding of what makes one a saint. In that system, a saint is someone very special and holy. They live a life of piety. They are so much purer than the everyday believer. Very few of us will ever be considered a saint. Saints are way up there, and we are way down here. We say things like, "Don't say that about my mother! She was a saint," meaning she was so good, better than most. This is not what makes a person a saint. A saint is every single believer. Every "called out one" is a saint. Jesus pulled us out of the world and into His family; that makes us saints. We can't make ourselves holy. We are holy and set apart because our Savior, Father, and the Spirit of God is holy and has established our holiness in Him. We are not godly, and that is the work we must commit ourselves to, to love and live with His heart and mind.

What is the problem? So many of us don't know who we are. We are unsure of His love for us, and we have a chink in our armor. We have an open back door that allows the devil to manipulate and keep us a prisoner to lies. When we agree that we are a sinner, we are probably going to act like one. Our identity is still in our old self, not in the new man. When we perceive ourselves as a sinner, we are going to sin. But, that does NOT change who you are - a child of God. It doesn't change your true identity. The Father communicates identity. When He sees you and me, He sees Jesus, His beloved Son. That is who we are; we are IN His Son. That makes us His eternal children, sons and daughters of the living God.

We wrestle with believing what Jesus did was enough. It was, and it is! Therefore, you must resist the devil and His lies, so you can step into who you already are in Him.

Later, we are going to look at the power of agreement. For now, I would just like to encourage you to consider this: What you agree with will become who you are and what you do. If you agree with the enemy's false identity defining who you are, you are going to continue to wrestle with sin. Remember, there is no fear in love. Jesus died for all your sin — including the sin you committed yesterday, last week, and ten minutes ago. He paid for it all. Just apologize and mean it, and jump into His loving arms. His arms are the safest place in the universe. The devil is not going to pursue you there. Trust me.

Holy Spirit is always going to speak God's truth and love to you. His role is never to punish you or put you down by telling you all you do wrong. Even when He speaks correction to discipline, it is always in love and builds up. Holy Spirit will NEVER tell you how small you are. He doesn't see you as small. He sees greatness in you. After all, you are His child. How can you be anything less than great?

I love this Kris Vallotton quote. It truly captures how God works in His love for us.

"God never reminds us of our smallness when He calls us to do something awesome. Instead He calls us to courage by proclaiming something amazing over us like, "You're a mighty warrior," "A father of many nations," or, "You're the one that all of Israel is waiting on!" Unlike God, the typical Christian culture embraces smallness to include people who feel insignificant." - Supernatural Ways of Royalty

I have always found it funny how the Lord called some of the great men of the Bible. My favorite might be Gideon. Here is Gideon, hiding in a winepress, sifting wheat, hiding himself and the wheat from the Midianites. The Angel of the Lord shows up and says, *"The Lord is with you, O mighty man of valor. Go in this might of yours and save Israel from the hand of Midian; do not I send you?"* I can almost picture Gideon looking at the Lord, looking over both shoulders and thinking, "Does He mean me? Are you talking to me? You can't be talking to me!" Gideon gives the angel all the reasons why he is not qualified. "Um, are you talking to me? I am no mighty man of valor, and what is this might that is mine? I may be many things, but brave and mighty? Nope, that isn't me. Do you see where I am? I am hiding here. Are you sure you don't mean my neighbor, Joe? He is big and strong, and he comes from the right pedigree."

We all know the rest of the story, but I am sure Gideon was quite surprised to be called a "man of valor." He hadn't done anything courageous; he was hiding. God sees us for who He made us to be. He will always call us out by speaking our true identity and destiny over us. He doesn't want us to be small and insignificant; there is no glory for Him in that. He wants us to walk in humility and in the power of His Spirit, advancing His Kingdom. He has "prepared good works for us," works that will bring Him glory and bring us fulfillment and joy.

No, you are not small sinners. You are saints, sons and daughters of the King of Kings, the Bride of Christ, princes and princesses of the Kingdom of Heaven. Stop listening to the lies, and start declaring the truth.

Go—empty the garage of all the garbage and clutter of your past, right up to this moment. All the lies, false self-images, everything that causes you shame. List it all out, give it to the Lord, and burn it to ashes. Every day, moment by moment, you have a choice. Will you choose to yield to fear, or will you choose love, run to your Father, trusting in His goodness and kindness towards you? He is good — perfectly good.

Remember, Holy Spirit will never affirm lies that have formed your identity outside of Christ. Holy Spirit always speaks to us the identity of sonship. It is sin to disagree with who God says you are. Take hold and contend for truth, and you will come to the place where you love and like yourself, even with all the bumps, bruises, scars, and moles. When you are able to love yourself, humbly receiving who the Holy Spirit says you are, you will be in a position to love others, even as the Lord loves them.

Section Four

The Two Kingdoms;

Their Culture, Economy, and

Attributes

Chapter 10
What is the Kingdom of God?

*Being asked by the Pharisees when the kingdom of God would come, he answered them, "The kingdom of God is not coming in ways that can be observed, nor will they say, 'Look, here it is!' or 'There!' for behold, **the kingdom of God is in the midst of you.**" Luke 17:20-21, NIV*

Just as there were two trees, and there are two fathers, there are also two kingdoms — the kingdom of darkness and the Kingdom of God. Both have cultural values, an economy, and resources, and each communicate a system to live by. They are complete opposites in every possible way. One kingdom has a righteous King. The other, a usurper, a despot, a murderer. One brings life, the other death. You cannot live in both kingdoms; to do so is to agree with a liar. Each kingdom carries its own atmosphere. One carries an atmosphere of light, life, and love. The other carries an atmosphere of darkness, death, and fear. We choose daily, even moment by moment, which we will live in and serve.

What makes a kingdom a kingdom? That is a good question. Our modern understanding of "kingdom" is rooted in the historical view of the last thousand years in Europe. The monarchies of the past do not offer a good understanding of what Jesus meant when He spoke of the Kingdom. Applying this perspective alone would lead us to a wrong conclusion. The modern understanding of a kingdom is the land and people over which a king exerts his authority. We see it in geographical terms. When we think of a kingdom today, we generally think of the Kingdom of Great Britain. There has been a royal family over the land for approximately 1300 years. Of course, the royal family has not actually had any ruling authority since The Reform Act of 1832.

At the same time, applying this concept of the Kingdom as simply a future inaugurated realm denies the scripture that says the Kingdom is present. This is where those fellow brothers and sisters that deny the gifts would stand. To apply this understanding to the spiritual realm, having God as head falls short of the true, biblical understanding. It is important for us to understand what Jesus meant by "the Kingdom of God," or the synonymous phrase "Kingdom of Heaven," if we are to understand the Father's intention for us. This understanding is central to the destiny of the Church. It is the faith of a son or daughter who has completely grasped hold of their identity as His child, who can release the power and authority of Christ in greater measure. This is our Father's desire, for us to walk in His power and authority, tearing down the works of the enemy, healing the sick, casting out demons, and setting captives free, in the name of His beloved Son, Jesus.

The ancient understanding of kingdom — the one more relevant for us — is more profound than the one we have looked at. Webster's Dictionary defines the archaic definition as the rank, quality, state, or attributes of a king; royal authority, dominion, monarchy, kingship. This understanding is rooted in the Hebrew word *malkuth* and the Greek *basileia*. They generally mean the rank, authority and sovereignty exercised by a king. *Basileia* would also include the realm in which His sovereign rule is exerted. According to the theologian George Eldon Ladd, "A kingdom is the authority to rule. The sovereignty of a king." (*The Gospel of the Kingdom: Scriptural Studies in the Kingdom of God, page 19*) When the Bible speaks of His Kingdom, it speaks of His sovereign rule, rather than simply a realm in which He rules. Why is this important? We need to understand that while our Father and King Jesus have a realm within creation, even if there was no realm, God would still be King. He doesn't need a realm to be King. He just is. It is not the realm that defines His authority, it is who He is.

Included in this understanding is the reality that we are His eternal children, called to rule and reign at the side of Jesus. "*For don't you know that you will judge angels... Do you not know that we are to judge angels?*" 1 *Corinthians 6:2-3.* Understanding the Kingdom from the perspective of Jesus opens a new understanding to who He is and who we are. Hebrews 1:3 tells us the universe is held together by the "word of His power." We seldom consider the power of God when He speaks into that which is not and creates. The Greek phrase theologians use for creation out of nothing is "*ex nihilo.*" It literally means to make something out of nothing. But in our case, we are something. We are something unique and precious. We are sons and daughters. When He speaks the word of His power, things shift. Scientists search for the power that holds everything together. What keeps the universe from falling apart? It is the Word of His power. In the beginning, God spoke, and power was released. It was the Logos speaking His Father's words, and the power released was beyond anything science can explain. They are looking for an energy, a force, a systematic organization of something that keeps us from flying apart. We know it is a person—Jesus! He is still speaking into us, forming us in His own image to the fullness of Christ Jesus. His word will never return void.

What does any of this have to do with us? We are now in Him. We are in the Word. We also carry within us the person of His Spirit. In Matthew 21:21, Jesus said, "If you have faith and do not doubt... you can say to this mountain, 'Go, throw yourself **into the sea**,' and it will be done." Certainly, He could speak and it would happen, but you or me? No way! Yet, when we know who we are and walk in the power of His faith as sons and daughters, *"greater things we will do."* We think it is our faith, but it is actually God's faith, by the Spirit within us, working through our faith in Him. It is only our lying identity that causes us to lack faith to enter into the power of the Kingdom and do all God would have us do.

The Kingdom is God's universal rule. While we may look around and see this planet, where almost nothing looks like what we imagine His rule to be, we can have confidence He is in control. He is in control, but He is not controlling. This simply means He works with our choices to bring us to the place He desires for us.

When we were "born again," we were promoted from sinner to saint, from orphan to a fully accepted, wholeheartedly and thoroughly loved son or daughter. We stepped into the possibility of experiencing a measure of His eternal Kingdom. We gained access to His Kingdom rule, accessible by His Spirit when we act according to His will. This is why Jesus tells us multiple times, "If you would only believe." His Kingdom is a realm in which He rules. It is His sovereign power causing all things to shift according to His good and perfect will. His desire is that His Kingdom would come, and His will be done here on earth as in Heaven. His will is that people come to the knowledge of God and be saved, that they would be healed and delivered from everything that afflicts them, so they would have joy in Him. He intends for that to happen—to a significant measure through His family. He calls us into Kingdom partnership to make it so.

When my oldest son, Jason, was nine to twelve years old, I worked restoring leather furniture. I loved it when he wanted to come to work with me. Not because he would help me get it done faster; truthfully, he usually made it take a little longer. I simply loved connecting with my son. Having him close to me, helping me was bonding, and hopefully, I taught him something of a work ethic. I loved having Jason with me, and I loved allowing him to find he could do more than he thought. Through helping me, I hoped to give both my sons something that would form them as men. God is much the same way. He calls us to exert His Kingdom power to do His Kingdom work, to form us as sons and daughters. His Kingdom is His sovereign power ruling, and He has invited us into His work for His glory.

Defining the Kingdom as only the people and land over which the King exerts authority brings us to a theological destination that leaves us without power. We are simply holding on until Jesus returns and rescues us. This diminishes access to the power Jesus released into the church at the Great Commission.

> *Jesus came and said to them, "All authority in heaven and on earth has been given to me. Go therefore and make disciples of all nations, baptizing them in the name of the Father and of the Son and of the Holy Spirit, teaching them to observe all that I have commanded you. And behold, I am with you always, to the end of the age."*
> *Matthew 28:18-20, ESV*

In the Great Commission, there is a Kingdom statement being made few of us take hold of. We focus on the evangelistic points: disciple the nations, baptize, teach. We miss one key point. He starts by saying, "All authority in Heaven and on earth has been given to Me." He already had ALL authority in Heaven, but now He has ALL authority here on earth. That means He has authority over every disease and every affliction of body, soul, and spirit. He has all authority over every single demon and even Satan himself. He has authority to release the Kingdom of Heaven upon the earth. How does a king exert his authority? By his word and by his servants. In the dynamic of Christ as King, He desires to do it through His body, His family, the Church. We take His Word, we live it, and we demonstrate it. We carry out His authority; this is how the Kingdom manifests around us. The Gospel of the Kingdom goes forth with both the declaration, His word, and the demonstration, His power.

The Kingdom of God is Not Just Words—It is Power

*And proclaim as you go, saying, "**The kingdom of heaven is at hand. Heal the sick, raise the dead, cleanse lepers, cast out demons** . . . " Matthew 10:7-8, ESV (emphasis mine)*

*And he said to them, "Go into all the world and proclaim the gospel to the whole creation. Whoever believes and is baptized will be saved . . . And **these signs will accompany those who believe: in my name, they will cast out demons; they will speak in new tongues; they will pick up serpents with their hands; and if they drink any deadly poison, it will not hurt them; they will lay their hands on the sick, and they will recover.**" Mark 16:15-18, ESV (emphasis mine)*

*Behold, **I have given you authority to** tread on serpents and scorpions, and over all the power of the enemy, and nothing shall hurt you. Luke 10:19, ESV (emphasis mine)*

175

My friends, Robby Dawkins and Brian Blount, live this out every day of their lives. They raised their children to live in the Kingdom, and they do the same. I have had the pleasure of doing several conferences with my buddy, Brian. I love this guy. His humility, passion, compassion, and courage to step through fear and love on strangers simply blows me away and challenges me. He gets it. He has led hundreds, if not thousands to the Lord, on three continents. Perhaps the best part of Brian and I's ministry is that we both love to activate people and let them loose. They always come back with great Jesus stories of healing and salvation. Love must multiply, and the Kingdom of God is all about love and multiplication.

For us to enter the future realm of God, we must give ourselves to trust in His power, authority, and Word, right now, moment by moment. When we do, with confidence in our sonship, we release the Kingdom in the present age. We will see cancer healed, the deaf hear, the lame walk, legs grow out, demons flee, and relationships restored.

Many years ago, my wife and I got a call from a family friend. Her daughter-in-law was dying of cancer and was in the final stages. She asked if we would come with her and pray for her daughter. Of course, we said yes. We drove the nearly two hours from Long Island to the hospital in New Jersey. When we got to her room, she looked terrible. Her skin and eyes were a deep yellow from the cancer. We found out the doctors only gave her days to live. Patti and I first prayed to the Lord, and then prayed for her, but nothing happened. We took a step back and talked with her a little more. We prayed again for the Kingdom to come and manifest. Almost immediately, we got a Word of Knowledge from the Lord regarding some unforgiveness towards a daughter and her mother. We explained what unforgiveness does. Right in the moment, her daughter walks in. We walked them through reconciliation. When they were done, with tears rolling down their faces, we led them both to the Lord. We prayed, and immediately, right in front of our eyes, the yellow in her eyes vanished as her corneas turned white. At the same time, her yellow skin turned a healthy white, complete with rosy cheeks. We saw it all in front of our eyes and believed she was completely healed. A couple of days later, we received a call from our family friend. She was excited. Her daughter-in-law was found to be cancer free. The day she was expected to die, she was released from the hospital. Over the next few weeks, her son and future daughter-in-law gave their lives to the Lord. This is the Kingdom. This is the rule and reign of God breaking through. It is the fulfillment of the Lord's Prayer, "Thy Kingdom come, Thy will be done, on earth as it is in Heaven."

The Attributes of the Kingdoms

For the kingdom of God is not a matter of eating and drinking, but of righteousness and peace and joy in the Holy Spirit. Romans 14:17, NIV

For the kingdom of God does not consist in talk but in power. 1 Corinthians 4:20, ESV

Jesus described His Kingdom as being present, yet future; revealed, yet a mystery; among us, yet not of this world; like a small seed, yet permeating everything. In Mark 1:15, *"The Kingdom of God is at hand,"* tells us the Kingdom is available now; it is within our reach. Matthew 21:43, *"Therefore I tell you, the kingdom of God will be taken away from you and given to a people producing its fruits,"* tells us the Kingdom must bear fruit. It must grow, multiply. Matthew 13:33, *"The kingdom of heaven is like leaven that a woman took and hid in three measures of flour, till it was all leavened,"* tells us the Kingdom is always at work and will continue to be until it takes over all.

The Kingdom of God is a Kingdom Founded in Love

Jesus answered, "The most important is, 'Hear, O Israel: The Lord our God, the Lord is one. And you shall love the Lord your God with all your heart and with all your soul and with all your mind and with all your strength.' The second is this: 'You shall love your neighbor as yourself.' There is no other commandment greater than these." Mark 12:29-31, ESV

As I said early on, God is love. The foundation of the universe is love. Not the emotion, but the power of an unbreakable love; the love that is a Person, the Godhead, the three-in-one.

The kingdom of darkness is the exact opposite of the Kingdom of God. Its foundation is fear. Fear permeates the kingdom of darkness. It exudes fear of all types. Everything from anxiety to terror is part of this kingdom, the purpose of which is to keep you blind to God and love. *All fear is of the devil.* The only exception is the fear that arises when real, carnal danger is present. All internal fear is from Satan. Just as love is the economy of Heaven, fear is the economy of darkness. The currency of fear is pride, insecurity, shame, envy, jealousy, bitterness, and strife. All things that destroy come from fear. Murder, addiction, strife, greed and covetousness, lying, theft, and bearing false witness all come from fear through pride, insecurity, shame, and anxiety.

What is pride? Pride is unhealthy self-love. It exalts itself above others. It builds an identity of self-importance, making oneself the center of all relationships. Pride in others is not what I am speaking of, nor the kind of pride that comes from doing something well. I am proud of my sons for the men they have become. God is proud of His children. Unhealthy pride is self-exaltation; it is the sin of Lucifer, the one who tried to exalt himself above God. Pride looks like arrogance, the opposite of humility.

Insecurity is a form of pride, in that insecure people want to draw others to themselves. Insecurity is self-doubt. It displays a lack of trust in the Lord. Insecurity causes us to want man's approval. The doubts that come with insecurity cover every area of life. It touches our relationships, our provision issues, and more. Most of all, insecurity causes man to question God's heart—His love, faithfulness, kindness, and goodness.

179

The truth is, we all wrestle with insecurity. It is not easily dealt with. It seeps out of us as unbelief, which kills faith. When the Lord tells us, "Seek first the Kingdom and ALL these things will be given to you," insecurity says, "I want to believe, but I can't." This causes us to strive and steals our peace. There is hope for victory; it is in taking hold of Christ and giving Him ALL areas of your life, especially your fears. Remember, "All things are possible through Christ Jesus."

I have already shared what shame is, but as a reminder, shame is self-hate. It is an identity we generally want to pity, but we need to kill our own shame. Shame is a stronghold assaulting the heart and mind to make the Father's love impotent. We must repent before God for hating who He loves. Shame causes us to keep running to false comforters. Shame says, "At my core, I am no good. I will fail. I am not worth loving." If the Father says you are worth His Son's death, who are you to say, "I am unworthy"? The worth of something is determined by the price someone is willing to pay for it. In our case, the greatest price possibly paid was paid at the Cross.

Anxiety is possibly the greatest struggle for people today. It seems to be the case for more woman than men, but both struggle with it. Anxiety is the fear of tomorrow, the fear of "what if." This is sin for a few reasons. First, it is an attempt to take control of your tomorrows. This is where the Lord says to have faith, to live for and enjoy today, and let Him take care of your tomorrows. We don't know what will happen tomorrow. I've had countless events in my life that came suddenly, both terrible and wonderful. I couldn't control any of them. My mom told me countless times growing up, "Don't worry about tomorrow. We will cross that bridge when we get there. Everything is going to work out. Just have faith." My whole life, she spoke these words to me and countless others. She had amazing faith the Lord would eventually come through, if we kept the faith, prayed, and stayed positive. Anxiety is the enemy of faith, hope, and peace. If you give into anxiety, I guarantee faith, hope, and peace will be weak or non-existent. It always comes back to "Trust in the Lord with all your strength, and lean not on your own understanding." This means lean into, rely on, and place your confidence in the Lord, not in your own reasoning or wisdom.

The problem is we all too often look at the times we were not well cared for. This is what the enemy wants. He has been working these pain points into our life for years. He builds a history that causes us to doubt God, not realizing it was our choice to believe a lie that cut off the blessing. After repentance, the next choice is to stop looking back.

My wife has been rear-ended a few times. The concern of it happening again has made her look in her rearview mirror a lot more. What would happen if she drove on the highway with her eyes fixed on the rearview mirror? You got it—she would crash. We all know we can't drive forward looking behind and not crash. It is guaranteed, yet so many of us go through life this way. We want to move forward with the Lord, but we are stuck looking backwards. The anxiety that rises is devastating.

Remember, the enemy wants you to crash and lose hope and faith in the Lord. Don't play his game.

This is where knowing the Word of the Lord is a weapon for us. I have a favorite scripture for those times, and thankfully, they are now very far and few between. Thank You, Jesus.

*The Lord is at hand; do not be anxious about anything, but in everything by prayer and supplication with **thanksgiving** let your requests be made known to God. **And the peace of God**, which surpasses all understanding, **will guard your hearts and your minds in Christ Jesus.***

*Finally, brothers, whatever is true, whatever is honorable, whatever is just, whatever is pure, whatever is lovely, whatever is commendable, if there is any excellence, if there is anything worthy of praise, **think about** these things. What you have learned and received and heard and seen in me — **practice** these things, and **the God of peace will be with you.***

Philippians 4:5-9, ESV (emphasis mine)

These verses are very powerful. When we apply these truths, we have a powerful weapon to overcome many areas of fear; particularly anxiety. The first weapon we are given is thankfulness. Thankfulness is powerful. Look at the Old Testament to see how many times they were told to remember what the Lord had done for them. Over and over, we hear things like, "Remember the Lord your God who led you out of Egypt, and provided manna in the desert," and so on. Why? If they would remember His goodness with a thankful heart, their faith was protected. Thankfulness would be a shield against hopelessness, unbelief, and more. Look at verse 7. It says "The peace of God... will guard your hearts and minds." When you remember Him with thankfulness, you position yourself inside His peace. Though there may be tumult outside, your heart rests in His goodness. When Paul says your heart and mind, he is speaking of your soul. The enemy hates a thankful believer.

The next section instructs us on how to enter this practice. We are told to consider several things in our life. We are to think and meditate on what is true, honorable, just, pure, lovely, and commendable. Another way to say it is to fix our thoughts on these things. These are the things that build up our souls. If we put this into practice, God manifesting as peace will be close to us.

Jeremiah 6:16 tells us, "*Thus says the Lord: Stand in the ways and see and ask for the old paths, where the good way is and walk in it; **then you will find rest for your souls**.*" When he says "stand, see, ask" for the "old paths," we are being instructed to remember the things we know, and remember the goodness of God. When we do, our souls, thoughts, emotions, and will rest in Him. He is our resting place, even as He has ordained we will be His resting place.

You may feel like life has been very painful, and you have very little to be thankful for. I have known people, and I am sure you do, too, that this has been their experience. If this is you, my heart goes out to you. If you absolutely can't find anything to hold onto, whether before or after you came to know Jesus, you can start with the knowledge that your name is written in "The Lamb's Book of Life." You are redeemed, and you will live for all eternity in the presence of love, where there is no more suffering, only joy and peace. Someone told me that once. I thought, "Yes, if I have nothing else, I am so thankful for that." You might find as you start there, you will see the Lord's hand working at other times, and you will be thankful.

As I said already, the economy of the Kingdom of God is exactly opposite the kingdom of darkness. The economy of the Kingdom of God is love. Just as fear releases a currency, so does love. The currency of love is the fruit of the Spirit: *joy, peace, patience, kindness, goodness, faithfulness, gentleness, self-control.* There is nothing that can come against the fruit of the Spirit. It is currency because these are things we get to spend on others to reveal love to them in ways that reveal God. There is also freedom because there is "no law," no religiosity or rule keeping. We are free!

Opposing Atmospheres

We don't hear much discussion in the Church around understanding spiritual atmospheres. Some may say it is not biblical. I would beg to differ. I teach a conference called "Understanding and Shifting Atmospheres." In it, I unwrap this topic over five one-hour teaching sessions. I believe if we come to understand this spiritual truth, we can be more intentional in our walk and ministry.

First, consider that the spiritual world is eternal and superior to the natural world. We live in a world that at best is a greatly inferior reflection of the eternal. I am not approaching this from a gnostic position; what we do here matters a lot. I am saying there are some things we walk in and carry that have a powerful effect.

First, let's consider the words for "spirit", both Hebrew and Greek, respectively. *Ruach* is the Hebrew word. It means a few different things, but the most common synonyms are "breath" and "wind." In the Greek, the word is *pneuma*. It carries the same primary understanding: "breath and wind, moving air." One of the names of Satan is Prince of the Power of the Air. We see the evidence of this "power of the air" in our media, entertainment, and anything going out over the "airwaves." The influence of the kingdom of darkness through the air is easily seen and experienced.

I am a prophetic feeler. I can feel a shift in the air in different ways, both good and evil. Several years ago, my wife and I went away for a long weekend. This is one thing we try our best to do, at least once a year. There is an inn we like in Rhinebeck, in upstate New York. We both like the Beekman Arms, though we like it for different reasons. My wife loves that the rooms all have vintage four poster beds with canopies. I love the fact it is the oldest working inn in America, and that Washington, Hamilton, Benedict Arnold, and others stayed there while preparing the troops for battle. I mean, they prepared their troops right on the front lawn of the inn, and the original pub is exactly as it was then. Pretty cool, right? It doesn't hurt that the bedrooms have fireplaces either. I love a nice fireplace. While visiting there one year, we decided to take a ride and cross over the Hudson River from the east side to the west. Once we crossed, we saw signs for Woodstock. We had never seen Woodstock, famous for the historic concert that was named after the town, though the rock festival didn't take place there. As we approached the town, I started to feel queasy. Once we entered the town, I was nauseous and getting sicker by the minute. I quickly discerned there was a strong spirit of witchcraft. I started looking at the stores. The town was filled with crystal, stones, shops, psychics, and other dark things. I got out of there fast, and as soon as I got out of the village, I was perfectly fine. On the way back, as we crossed the Hudson, we came to a town called Skaneateles, New York. It seemed like a nice little town, so we got out of the car to explore, and immediately, I felt peaceful. We spent a few hours looking at antiques. We had lunch and left thinking it was a nice town. About six months later, a visiting minister came to a church we have friendship with. As he was sharing a little about himself, he tells the congregation he is from Skaneateles. After the meeting, I shared my experience and how good I felt in his town. He told me the Woodstock area does indeed have a strong influence of witchcraft. When he shared about his town, he told me why I experienced such a stark difference. He said, "You know why it was so different? The last several years, a dozen churches have come together every Monday. We prayer walk the town, asking the Lord to seal it and asking for His presence to rest on our city." This story shows how atmospheres work, and how both kingdoms carry an atmosphere.

Not only do towns, regions, and countries carry atmospheres, people do as well. Have you ever been in one mood, encounter someone else, and your entire mood shifts? You probably came into their atmosphere. I have experienced this in both directions, good and bad. I have been in a dark place emotionally, and come into the atmosphere of love or peace, and suddenly the darkness was gone. I have also experienced the other side of this, where I was feeling pretty good, and suddenly I feel anxious or angry, or another negative emotion. I have trained myself to be aware, and to take a moment to check to see if it is me or someone else. My close friend, Dan, who travels with me when I speak, is super sensitive to atmospheres. There have been times we are walking through an airport and I am talking to him, and suddenly, he is gone. I turn around, and he is leaning on a wall, or sitting hunched in a chair. I ask, "What's going on?" He says, "Someone is really angry," or "Someone has a lot of anxiety," or whatever is going on. One time, we were driving to pray for someone in the hospital. Dan was driving, and suddenly his head jerks. He grabs his neck and says, "Ouch!" I asked, "What is going on?" He said, "Somebody is very angry." In less than a minute, a car flies by way us well over the speed limit, weaving dangerously through traffic. Dan says, "There he goes!

Wow. That is much better." Dan experienced the driver's atmosphere.

If you look at the culture of a country, region, or even a city, you can identify the atmosphere. Except for one year in my late teens, I have never lived further than ninety minutes from New York City. Needless to say, I am very familiar with NYC. When we look at the wealth in New York City, and the power coming from there, we can easily see the atmosphere of greed, power, and lust. You don't need to be overly sensitive to see the influence of these things. Along with this atmosphere there is one of anxiety, you can feel it tangibly as you get closer to the city. Don't get me wrong, New York is an amazing city filled with culture, the best food in the world, shows, museums, and history as well. But it has a distinct atmosphere.

This gives you some understanding of the big picture of atmospheres. Let's talk a bit about personal and corporate atmospheres. Let's look at 2 Samuel 19, the story of Saul sending men to capture David. In the story, they keep encountering a band of prophets. Every time one comes near them, the Holy Spirit comes upon them to prophesy, until Saul himself comes, strips naked, and prophesies. Keep in mind, the Spirit of the Lord is like the wind. The Spirit has an atmosphere, and the anointing is an atmosphere. As they entered the corporate anointing flowing from the presence of the Spirit of God, the atmosphere came over them, and they prophesied. In Acts 5, we have the story of how the Spirit was moving through the Apostles. In verse 15, "...*they even carried out* *the sick into the streets and laid them on cots and mats, that as Peter came by at least **his shadow** might fall on some of them."* There was something that happened when the shadow of Peter touched sick people. They identified the power with his shadow; it was just as likely the atmosphere of the Spirit's presence released the healing. Peter spent so much time in the Word, prayer, and the presence of the Lord, the anointing was thick on him. Jesus had experiences where He didn't touch anyone, and their faith healed them. They entered the atmosphere of Jesus and of Peter, and the anointing and faith activated the healing power. We are spirit beings, and we carry an atmosphere. What will our atmosphere be? Remember the character Pigpen from Charlie Brown? He never washed or cleaned his clothes. In the comics and the holiday specials, wherever he went, he brought a dirt cloud with him. That was Pigpen's atmosphere. We all have walked into a place of worship and felt the weightiness of the Lord's presence. We have stepped into Heaven's atmosphere. Likewise, in deliverance ministry, you often feel the dark atmosphere of the demon present.

Atmospheres are real. They influence for good or evil, and our spirit and soul can have reactions to them. It is important to understand this. If you do, you can be intentional in your personal prayer life and when you are ministering to others. It is also important to protect your own soul while you walk through life. I taught on this at my church one Sunday. The following week, one of my friends in the congregation shared a testimony. She said she was doing some shopping and was in a very good mood. She went into a store to pick up a few things, and within a few minutes, she started to feel tired and agitated with all the people crowding in the store. After a few moments, she remembered what I shared on Sunday. She decided to test it. She found an empty aisle and said something like, "I am a daughter of the King—a Jesus follower. You have no right to affect me. I rebuke you in Jesus' name. In fact, while I am here, you can't do this anymore." She said she was immediately back in a great mood. A few aisles over, she saw someone with a cane. She asked if she could pray for her, and the pain left the woman, and she didn't need the cane. What happened? Had she stayed under the influence of the atmosphere, she probably would not have prayed for that person. She would have gotten what she needed, paid, and left. Instead, she brought the atmosphere of Heaven, acting in the authority she had in Jesus as a daughter. This is a great practical story of discerning the atmosphere and shifting it.

What shifts atmospheres? The same things that draw presence. Worship, prayer, good works, speaking the Word, speaking in tongues, and prophecy can all shift an atmosphere. Whenever we intentionally make space for the Holy Spirit, we have stepped into the authority to shift atmospheres.

One word of caution: It is important to understand what you have authority to shift and what you do not. As "born again" believers, we have authority to speak into and shift anything that comes into the realm of earth. The earth is where we have authority. Any spiritual dynamic that directly touches you or those around you, you have authority to rebuke and assert your authority in Christ. As far as the influences over regions, cities, and communities, you intercede to the Lord asking Him to shift the atmosphere and it's influences. It is important to understand where our authority begins and ends. This will keep us out of a lot of trouble.

Honor vs. Dishonor

We were made for community. We were made to be part of a family. Every person longs for a place to belong. I have never seen a believer stay outside of consistent community connection and grow in the way they would in healthy community. By design, we need the iron of relationship sharpening the iron of character. I understand we can get hurt in the Church, even badly hurt. I was part of a church for twelve years that lived in a measure of spiritual abuse, of which I was one of the prime victims. I understand the pain of those situations and have compassion for those who have suffered in this way. While my family and I had to walk through the pain of that season and be healed from the sense of betrayal and abandonment, we've had the privilege of helping many who have been under the false authority of spiritual abuse find freedom. We forgave and because we forgave and prayed in love, we gained authority and wisdom to help others. Choosing to receive the Father's love moved us past the pain. We made a choice to allow the process of healing form Christ in us. Being hurt by churches, no matter how many times, is not a reason to abandon community. Isolation is dangerous. We simply need to find the right community, while understanding there is no perfect place. You want to find a place where people are honored, where the leaders are approachable and correctable, and humble enough to admit when they are wrong. Though we may not like it, finding love always has a measure of risk. If we continue risking in love, we will find it. If we withdraw from the risk, I guarantee you will not find the love that brings life.

Living lives of honor is a high priority to the Lord. The sons and daughters of God should be pressing into a lifestyle of honor. When we do, we reflect Him more fully. This is not easy. We don't see a lot of honor around us. Models of true, biblical honor are hard to find. All over the news, we see dishonor. This is not surprising because the enemy fuels the life that dishonors. Honor is about loving, selfless service. Dishonor is about selfish, self-seeking self-promotion. If honor is what love looks like in community, dishonor is what fear, pride, and insecurity look like in community. In Genesis chapter 9, we have the story of Noah planting a vineyard. In this story, Noah made some wine and drank too much. He apparently falls asleep from drinking too much. Ham sees his dad naked in the tent and runs to tell his brothers. Either Ham thought it was funny, or thought it was a terrible display by his father. Either way, he was wrong. Instead of honoring his father and keeping it to himself, he runs to expose him. When Ham tells his brothers, Japheth and Shem, instead of further exposing their father, they take a garment, walk in backwards so they don't see the shameful state of their father, and cover him with the garment. They covered Noah in his weak, vulnerable and embarrassing state. This story is a great example of honor.

Many years ago, when we were planting our church, I had a leader whose spouse was very angry with me, on and off for probably two years. They felt it was dishonoring that I failed to say hello when they first came to church on Sunday mornings. They saw my lack of recognizing them and saying hello before the service as ignoring them. I tried to explain that on Sunday morning before the service, I had a lot going on. At the time, I was leading worship, preaching, and praying in preparation for the service. I pointed out, I always said hello after the service and spent time with them. That was not good enough. I assured them I was not ignoring them. "I have tunnel vision ten minutes before service, making sure everything is ready to go. I am sorry, but I don't even see you. Ignoring you would mean I see you and make a choice not to recognize you. I am not doing that. It is just part of my wiring. I focus on the tasks and all that needs to be done in preparation for the service. I am sorry you have been hurt. That is not my heart towards you."

One evening around 8:30 p.m., the husband calls and blasts me—profanity, judgment, and rage. I let him ramble on for about ten minutes. Then I said, "This is not the time or the way to have this conversation." I politely said goodbye. A few days later, I get a call, and he is very chipper. All is good, and he tells me he feels much better. I told him it wasn't that simple. "We need to have a talk.

You bring someone with you, and my co-pastor will be there as well. We met, and I listened for an hour as he went over my failing to acknowledge them five minutes before the service begins. After about an hour, my co-pastor was ready to jump in with a bit of his own business. Afterwards, he told me he didn't understand why I would put up with that for an hour. I told him the goal of conflict for me is not to determine who is right. It is to demonstrate honor with accountability and to land on love so all parties can move forward. I want to hear the heart, be sure I understand what is really going on, ponder until I hear the Lord, and respond wisely.

As we approached an hour, I was getting a bit frustrated with it all. We couldn't get past the perception of ignoring, as opposed to my tunnel vision when I have so much on my mind. As I turned my heart and mind towards the Lord, I asked, "Lord, what do I do to model honor, love, and protect the relationship honestly?" Immediately, the Lord reminded me of boxing. I used to love boxing and watching boxing. My dad was a black belt in Judo and taught me about self-defense. I said to this irate friend, "Have you ever watched a boxing match?" "Yes," he replied. "If a boxer has a badly bruised and bleeding eye, and he is my adversary, I am going to attack him from the blind side. I will take advantage of his weakness to my own advantage. But if you and I are friends, and we are in a street fight, and you have a bad eye, I am going to stand and fight on your blindside. I will protect the side where your vision is impaired. You have a choice; you can keep punching me on my blind side, or you can protect me on my blind side. Which would you rather do?" I asked. "How do I do that?" he asked. "When I walk past someone before the service and I don't say hello, come and tell me I missed someone. Then, I can go say hello. You have now helped me where I am weak. You protected me." He responded, "Oh, that's simple. I can do that." I apologized again that their feelings were hurt, and he apologized for the inappropriate phone call. That was the end of it.

What I want you to see from this story is that honor doesn't seek to be right. Honor is always looking for a way to bring truth in love, building relationship and maintaining connection. Though I was the pastor, I didn't see that as making me better than him. Listening and not reacting, along with pondering, allowed me to hear the Lord and respond with wisdom, kindness, and love. Honor is not an award or a reward. Honor is an action of love that builds up, protects, and maintains connection. Honor seeks the truth, and acts in a way that reveals truth, while maintaining people's dignity. You don't lie to protect the relationship; that would be dishonoring and destructive. Instead, you address it straightforwardly, with patience, integrity, and kindness, as best as you can. That is not to say you allow yourself to be anyone's punching bag. That is dishonoring yourself. You are more valuable than that. There will be times you need to say, "This is not getting us anywhere. Perhaps it is best we both simply move on and go our own way. I love you, but this cannot keep going this way. It is not acceptable or healthy for us or for others."

Honor lifts others up onto your shoulders and helps them step into their gifts. Honor is never threatened by another's gifting. When honor encounters those more gifted, it finds joy and purpose in coming alongside, encouraging, and building up. Honor understands love is the priority, and when we love and honor well, we glorify our Father and our Savior. That is the priority of honor.

Dishonor, on the other hand, seeks to expose to build themselves up. People of dishonor tend to be gossip mongers, hearsayers, self-promoting, and double-minded. The Bible is full of people that were dishonoring. One obvious individual is Judas Iscariot. He had no honor. He had his own agenda, didn't think through the ramifications of his choices, and betrayed Jesus for money.

Paul, in Philippians 2:3-8, gives us the perfect definition of honor:

> **Do nothing from selfish ambition or conceit, but in humility count others more significant than yourselves. Let each of you look not only to his own interests, but also to the interests of others.** Have this mind among yourselves, which is yours in Christ Jesus, who, **though he was in the form of God, did not count equality with God a thing to be grasped, but emptied himself, by taking the form of a servant,** being born in the likeness of men. And being found in human form, he humbled himself by becoming obedient to the point of death, even death on a cross.

This is an amazing scripture. Paul is telling us how to live in a way that reveals Christ, how to honor the Lord. Do nothing from selfish ambition. Notice he doesn't say ambition in general, but selfish ambition. It is good to be ambitious for Jesus. This is the type of ambition Hudson Taylor had—leaving his family in England to go to China with nothing but an ambition to reach the Chinese for Jesus. He knew he probably would never see his loved ones again. He chose to be a servant of Christ. This is good ambition. Selfish ambition is all about us; it is an evil ambition rooted in pride.

Be humble, considering others more significant than yourself. This doesn't mean put yourself down. It means lift others up, without lifting yourself up. Let God promote you. We live this out as we look out for those around us.

Paul goes on to say, Jesus, the eternal One, didn't hold on to that identity, but humbled Himself to the point of dying on the Cross, being a servant of all. Do you realize when Jesus did that, He demonstrated how much He valued all of us? He demonstrated honor towards all people, not simply those that would believe in Him. He died once for ALL. He honored you and me in this selfless, sacrificial act.

Look at Jesus washing the feet of the disciples. Have you ever noticed Judas, the one who would betray Him just a couple of hours later, was present and would have his feet washed by the Master? Jesus teaches his disciples the last lesson He wants them to have before He goes to the Cross.

When he had washed their feet and put on his outer garments and resumed his place, he said to them, "Do you understand what I have done to you? You call me Teacher and Lord, and you are right, for so I am. If I then, your Lord and Teacher, have washed your feet, you also ought to wash one another's feet. For I have given you an example, that you also should do just as I have done to you." John 13:12-15, ESV

Jesus, the King, the eternal King, is on His knees with a large towel wrapped around His waist, washing His disciples' dirty feet, even the one He knows is about to betray Him. This is the perfect display of honor.

Honor protects, builds up, and speaks the truth in selfless love. Honor pursues truth. Honor always chooses righteousness and love. Honor serves without expectation of anything in return. Because it has a high value for honest, intimate, healthy, authentic relationship; honor is fearless in brave communication. Honor doesn't bow its knee to pride, fear, or arrogance. The selfless nature of honor builds powerful communal bonds that can weather every battle and be made stronger for it. Jesus is the highest model for relational honor.

Chapter 11
The Power of Agreement

Now faith is the assurance of things hoped for, the conviction of things not seen. For by it the people of old received their commendation. By faith we understand that the universe was created by the word of God, so that what is seen was not made from things that are visible. Hebrews 11:1-3, ESV

Every day of our life we make agreements. When you go to a store and make a purchase, you have made an agreement. The item you purchased had a price. That price was the value of what you were about to purchase. There is an unspoken agreement. The store made a proposal: if you want this, this is what it costs. When you purchased the item, you fulfilled an agreement. This is true of everything we purchase. Agreements define a relationship between two or more parties who have agreed to certain parameters, values, and guidelines for the relationship. When two people come to a conclusion, both approve, and there is an agreement. We do this in relationships all the time, though we don't realize that is what we are doing. When my wife wants a paint color for the living room I don't care for, and I have a color she doesn't care for, we look at colors until we find one we both like. When we make the decision together, we have an agreement. If I go speak in another part of the country and return to find the color we agreed to was not used, we have a broken agreement. Agreements are part of our daily life.

Faith and fear function in the same way. Hebrews 11:1 defines faith as, "*the assurance of things hoped for, the conviction of things not seen.*" Faith is the activation of two things—hope with conviction. When hope and belief line up, we activate faith to attain the thing we hope for. In the same chapter, in verse 3, we are told the universe, everything within creation, was made by faith. You mean even God must have faith to do what He desires to do? Absolutely! It is God-faith that makes all things happen according to His will. He is in us, therefore God-faith is in our spirit by Holy Spirit. The only difference between us and God is He doesn't have any doubt. Think about this. There is nothing, and the Trinity have a conversation. The Father says to Holy Spirit and the Logos (pre-incarnate Christ), "I want us to create together." The Father explains to the Son, "I want You to speak into the nothingness everything that is in My heart. Holy Spirit, when the Son speaks, You will release the power to make it so." We, you and I, have all the elements present needed for faith to create. We are in agreement with something that is not the present state, something God wants but we can't see. But we do have hope and conviction that what He desires, He is capable of doing. He will make it so. We have both the One, with hope and conviction, speaking out from agreement, and the One who makes it so. We are simply the conduit for His will to be done. This is how all healing and miracles work. When we agree with the Lord, "All things are possible with God," and "Everything is possible for one who believes." Faith is wholehearted agreement with God, according to His will, with conviction and hope, unhindered by our human perception. His reality is superior to ours, we are confident of this truth. When we live in this way, anything is possible. James tells us, *"You do not have because you do not ask God. When you ask, you do not receive, because you **ask with wrong motives.**"* This verse tells us faith is activated by asking with conviction, along with unselfish motives. When belief and hope line up with appropriate action, faith is released. Since those of us who are "born again" have the Holy Spirit in us, we can ask for anything with right motives and expect an answer.

As we have already seen, it was faith, God's faith, that created everything seen and unseen by the power of His Word, the Logos, the pre-incarnate Jesus, and the moving of the Holy Spirit. The exact same mechanism for all healing, deliverance, and the miraculous works the same way through us. We are now "in Christ," and the Holy Spirit is in us. When we speak healing, or any other miraculous work, knowing it is the heart of God to do what we ask, it becomes as if the Son is asking, and the Spirit moves to make it so. When we ask in His name, it is as if Jesus Himself is making the request, as we are in Him. The key to all of this is asking unselfishly, not from self-serving, and asking with confidence that what we ask for is in God's heart to do. His will be done!

A lack of understanding of faith causes so many Jesus followers to live in less than what is available for them. Wherever I travel, I routinely hear prayers that are more pleading for the Lord to move than a declaration of faith. I hear people say things like, "Lord, would You heal so-and-so, if it is Your will. Lord, would You please do this…" These are not prayers of faith, and they are not the biblical model. We have been taught in many places that sickness, afflictions of all kinds, and pain in general is, at the very least, at times from God; it must be His will. That is a lie. God is not the author of pain, sickness, suffering, and death. We read things like Paul sharing his "thorn in the side" and the Spirit telling him, "in your weakness Christ is perfected" to mean that God sent the suffering. We look at Jesus saying to Peter, "Satan has asked to sift you," as God being the cause. Yes, perhaps the Lord gives the go-ahead, always with a good purpose, but that doesn't mean He intends useless suffering. The Lord allows suffering to form us in His image or bring us to repentance. Allowing and causing are not the same thing. We live in a fallen world, and Satan and our flesh still have the right of involvement where we give permission. When we fully understand agreement, we will see that far too often, we bring these things upon ourselves.

Most of the men and women I know who see healing regularly never ask if it is God's will to heal. Anyone that denies the scripture in this area does not fully understand Matthew 10:8, Luke 9:1-2, Luke 10:9, and especially Mark 16:15- 18 as follows.

He said to them, "Go into all the world and preach the gospel to all creation. Whoever believes and is baptized will be saved, but whoever does not believe will be condemned. And these signs will accompany those who believe: In my name, they will drive out demons; they will speak in new tongues; they will pick up snakes with their hands; and when they drink deadly poison, it will not hurt them at all; they will place their hands on sick people, and they will get well."

Notice, Jesus does not say, "those who follow Me in this generation." He doesn't say, "until those who have seen Me are gone." He says, *"whoever believes and is baptized… these signs will go with them."* This tells me we should expect to see these things occur through our lives. We should "ALL" experience healing when we pray for people. We should all cast out demons. Yes, there is a learning curve, and it is good to get equipped, but I can tell you, the first miracles I saw through my own prayer, I had no training. I saw this verse and took it as the Word of God. I saw cancer healed, scoliosis healed, a damaged eye healed, cartilage damage in a knee healed, and someone with acute angina, with a nitroglycerin patch over his heart, completely healed. Now, 31 years later, he has never had to wear a patch again, he is angina free, and has no heart issues whatsoever. I can say this with confidence because he is my oldest brother, Jessie. I saw these healings before I had any formal training. All I had was a Bible and faith I could take it at it's word. That is all we need to see the miraculous. I still believe that today and continue to see miracles.

Before we wrap up this topic, let's talk about fear. While faith is the power that releases the Kingdom breakthrough, fear is the power that chains people to darkness. Faith and fear are complete opposites, but both work according to the same spiritual dynamics. Whereas faith is the power of hope with conviction, fear is the power of doubt, unbelief, and hopelessness with conviction. Faith works through agreement with the Lord and His truth. Fear is agreement with the enemy and his lies. Faith releases life, and fear releases death.

When we agree with one or the other, we position ourselves to receive the economy of that kingdom. Whichever we agree with, we position ourselves to release the atmosphere of that kingdom. What does this mean? When we agree with the truth of the Word of the Lord, we position ourselves under His grace. With His grace comes love, life, truth, peace, and joy. When we agree with fear, we come under the products of fear: anxiety, doubt, unbelief, resentment, bitterness, envy, and jealousy. Fear draws with it the things of the kingdom of darkness: physical, relational, emotional, and financial death. Death came through Adam's agreement with the devil. Life comes by our agreement with Jesus and His Word. Do not misunderstand what I am saying here. I am not saying when fear overwhelms a believer, they are going to lose relationship with the Lord. If they give into fear, they will most likely have great difficulty experiencing the Father's love. The fact that you may not experience His love doesn't mean He stopped loving you; His love is unbreakable. It simply means your soul can't recognize or take hold of His love. This is easily repaired through repentance and a change in language and thought.

Since fear and faith both work by agreement, it is important to watch our thoughts and our words, as well as our emotions. Faith is agreement combined with a strong belief for all Jesus has made available to us. Fear is the certainty of receiving that which we do not want. When our thoughts, emotions, and words agree with fear, the very thing we fear, we draw near. What we speak has power. All that God has done came by His spoken words. *"Let there be light! Lazarus, come forth! Be healed!"* Our spoken word has power and authority to release into our life. Fear and faith carry atmospheres. The primary atmosphere in the kingdom of darkness is fear. This atmosphere carries all other atmospheres of darkness. The atmosphere of the Kingdom of God is love. Faith flows from love — not the emotion, but the relational connection and confidence that comes with intimacy with God. Faith is powerful because it is rooted in the knowledge of God's love and goodness; it releases the confidence to believe in all His promises, moving us to declaration and action causing the Kingdom to manifest. When we struggle with faith, we are struggling with our confidence in His love.

When we yield to fear, there can only be one response: repentance, turning back to Jesus. Fear and Jesus can't coexist in the same space. Light destroys darkness. We repent, and we take hold of His truth in our speech and thoughts. How? Speak His Word out loud. Find scripture that speaks the opposite of the fear we are wrestling with. We worship by setting the eyes of our heart on Him in surrender. Remember His promises for those who are His, and remember His personal promises others have spoken into our life. When we get prophetic words, it is good to record them on a phone or write them down. They became weapons in our hands to declare His personal promises over our life. Most importantly, *stop agreeing with your fears.* What you set your focus on, you attract into your life. Paul is pointing to this in Philippians 4:8-9.

"Finally, brothers and sisters, whatever is true, whatever is noble, whatever is right, whatever is pure, whatever is lovely, whatever is admirable – if anything is excellent or praiseworthy – think about such things . . . And the God of peace will be with you." Philippians 4:8-9.

When we think in fearful ways, we position ourselves under the atmosphere of darkness. We draw the oppression and depression that comes with it, along with its other attributes: bitterness, resentment, and anxiety. Paul is telling us, "Watch your thought life. It is powerful. If you focus on the things that build up—the truth—the very God of peace will draw near to you." It sounds so simple, but it is not. It comes with a battle, but a battle already won if you can step into who you are and who your God is. Remember, He is good. Always and forever good.

Every day, we have situations that test the foundation our lives are built upon. Every human has a foundation of love or fear. Some of us have a mixed foundation and are constantly battling the two. This is only because you have not fully accepted that you are thoroughly loved and perfectly righteous in Christ. This is still true for Christians. While we have already been redeemed, we are in process. Much of this process is focused on agreements, or making better choices based on His love and truth: His truth about Himself and His truth about you; His truth about people and His truth regarding the values and culture of the world. When we are in the habit of agreeing only with Him, there is no force that can stop us from stepping into all He has for us. This battle is all about agreements. It is the Father's plan that we become just like Jesus. Jesus never had a moment where the choices in front of Him were ever opened to doubt. He knew who His Father was, and He knew who He was. He lived out of the conviction that His Father was good, loving, and trustworthy *always*. Circumstances were not powerful enough to sway Him from the conviction of the goodness of God. Not the persecutions and cruelty of men. Not the betrayal and abandonment of friends. Not 39 lashes from a cat o' nine tails ripping at His flesh. Not even the Cross or silence of God. He knew His Father was perfect in goodness and love. He knew who He was. He knew His Father's promise that He would be raised on the third day. He trusted His Father's promise for His destiny; through Him the children would come home. He rested in truth. He overcame darkness. He is enthroned in glory forever. Glory to God!

Section Five

The Father's Intention;

Shifting Our Paradigm

Chapter 12
The Father's Intention

... let us run with endurance the race that is set before us,
*looking to Jesus, the founder and perfecter of our faith, **who***
for the joy that was set before him endured the cross,
despising the shame, and is seated at the right hand of the
throne of God. Hebrews 12:1-2, ESV

All creation was made for the joy and glory of the
Father. Jesus was so devoted to the fulfillment of the
Father's joy realized, He laid everything down to go to the
Cross. Everything the Son did, from the first, "Let there
be," to "It is finished" and beyond, to the end of the age,
is for the joy of His beloved Father. Our ultimate destiny,
our reason for being, is wrapped in this truth: it's all for
the Father's great joy. It is the Father's desire to have
children. It is the Father's desire for His Son to have a
Bride. It is the Father's desire He would have a resting
place for His Spirit in us. Our role has been a mystery. It
doesn't make sense until we grasp who we truly are.
What does it really mean to be a son or daughter of God?
That is one really big question. The answer is wonderful,
mysterious, powerful, and life-changing; it has eternal
impact.

Identity as sons and daughters is critical to living
lives in the fullness of His intention, for His glory.

Understanding the two fathers, the two kingdoms, and the atmospheres and economies of each kingdom is critical for us to live in joy and walk out the victorious life we have in Christ Jesus. It is important we understand how the enemy relentlessly seeks to confuse us through fear and lead those astray that are seeking the Kingdom. From the beginning, he has been a liar, thief, and murderer.

Ephesians 1

When we read the Bible, it can often seem like God had a plan, but man, through Adam and Eve, messed it all up. I mean, really messed it up and everything else with it. It was so bad, we had to be kicked out of Eden before we ate the Tree of Life and permanently messed it up, with no hope of the situation ever being fixed. Ever since then, we have been trying to get it right, and God is trying to get us right, so we can go to Heaven. The only way God could fix it was to execute Plan B: send His Son to die for us. It's as if when Adam bit the apple, the Godhead responded with, "Wait a minute. Did you see that? Did you see what just happened? Did you see that coming? I didn't! What are we going to do now? I wasn't prepared for that, I'm not sure. Don't look at me, neither was I. I got it! Son, You are going to take on the flesh of man, die the worst, most horrific, painful death. Whoever believes You died for them, they get to come and join us. Okay, Father. But is that really the best we can come up with? Sorry, but yes. Okay, let's do it." I know this sounds silly, and we wouldn't say anything this absurd, but if we are honest, we would agree that some form of this is how we have thought at some point in our lives. It is understandable.

We have felt like we really blew it in the Garden, and it has all gone downhill from there, until Jesus. Now that we have Jesus, we need to work really hard not to lose Jesus, disappoint Him, or make Him angry. We must get everything right. The problem is, this thinking causes people to live in religious bondage, fear, anxiety, guilt, and shame.

Next, we have been told we are broken. Something is broken, and that is true. However, since the Lord weaved grace into His creation, and there was never anything but Plan A, we can safely assume everything is going to work together as He wills. Are you saying this horror we see all around us is God's will? Some might say yes, because God is in control of everything, nothing happens unless it is His will. Others would say no, we have free will, and we created this mess. My answer to both would be yes. God is fully in control, while at the same time, not controlling. We have the freedom to choose for ourselves, and at the same time, God is working "all things together for the good of those who love Him." That seems like semantics, but that is not the case. We can have free will to make our choices for good or for evil, and God can still cause things to work according to His plan. He doesn't control us. He is able to position Himself in the midst of our choices to bring forth His purposes for our lives. How is that not controlling? If this is the case, why does He allow suffering?

If we are to understand the answer to these questions, we need to start by answering this question: What is God's will for man? We have been told when we give our life to Jesus, everything changes. That is true on the inside; everything is different. On the outside, that isn't necessarily the case. For about six months, and maybe a year for some, we have a wonderful honeymoon with Jesus. However, that is not where we live for long. That is not to say it isn't all good; that is an understatement. Once He establishes our relationship in love, He begins to do what He purposes to do. He begins the work of forming us into the likeness of His Son. He begins dealing with our stuff: our sin, our inappropriate affections, everything getting in the way of transparency, vulnerability, truth, and love. Everything hindering transformation. We find in time, obedience is hard, and we inevitably come to places of choosing. Are we really going to bow to His will? What is His will? I thought it was to save me. I thought it was to help me be happy. Our happiness here is not the Father's highest purpose for us. His will is that we would be exactly like Jesus in every way; we would love like Jesus, carry the wisdom of Jesus, and walk in the power and authority of Jesus. We are on a journey of reformation from the inside out until we are filled to the fullness of Christ. That is the journey He intended from the beginning, and from the beginning, He provided all we needed.

*For he chose us in him before the creation of the world to be
holy and blameless in his sight. In love he predestined us for
adoption to sonship through Jesus Christ, in accordance with
his pleasure and will — to the praise of his glorious
grace, which he has freely given us in the one he
loves. Ephesians 1:4-6, NIV*

Paul is revealing a powerful truth: We were chosen
in Christ before anything was made. God willed we
would be "in" Christ from before the forming of creation,
we would become one with Him. Grace was woven into
the fiber of creation. We are living IN the grace of the
Father. In Revelation 13:8, the angel says, *"Everyone whose
name has not been **written before the foundation
of the world in the book of life of the Lamb who
was slain."** Jesus is the Lamb that was slain. This Book of
Life of the slain Lamb was present before the foundation
of the world was set. The provision for salvation was
present from the beginning. Nothing was left to chance.
All we need to do is surrender to Christ and take hold of
what has been provided through the Cross. The Cross is
the door. The Cross needs to bring us to the Resurrection.
It is at the Cross we begin to appropriate the fullness of
God, becoming a new man, a son or daughter of God.

Several years ago, I took a class on tape on the
doctrine of the Trinity, by Dr. Arthur Waeterling. It was a
brilliant teaching. When sharing on the second Person of
the Trinity, the pre-incarnate Jesus, he asked this
question, "If God is in everything, and there is no place
we can go in creation where He is not, and we carry sin,

and sin is darkness, and in God there is only light, how does sin exist in His Presence?" He gave this answer: Christ was the sin offering from before the foundation of creation. Always, the Logos, the Son, was the sacrifice for sin. The grace for salvation was built into creation. Creation is saturated with the grace that comes through the Lamb. This grace is the reason man was not obliterated in the Presence of a Holy God. There was no Plan B—there never was. It has always been Plan A. He is good, we are the object of His love and desire, and He left nothing to chance. His intention was too important, too dear to His heart to risk losing us.

Paul goes on to make several amazing statements as he continues his letter to the Ephesians. This grace that forgives our sin has been *lavished* on us in Christ. The word "lavished" means "to be poured out without measure, to be heaped upon, to be smothered in." Mary modeled this amazing grace when she anointed Jesus' feet; she poured out the oil extravagantly. God's grace for us is overflowing in and over our lives, and we are dripping in grace. Through Jesus and in Jesus, this beautiful gift of love has been and continues to be extravagantly poured into our lives. We need only appropriate it through faith, by resting in His goodness, kindness, and perfect will for our lives.

With all wisdom and understanding, he made known to us the mystery of his will according to his good pleasure, which he purposed in Christ, to be put into effect when the times reach their fulfillment — to bring unity to all things in heaven and on earth under Christ. Ephesians 1:8-10, NIV

In Christ, the Father's plan from the beginning was to bring all things into unity, harmony. All of creation — what we can see, and what we can't presently see — will be brought into oneness in Christ. We participate in this as His Body.

*It has been testified somewhere, **what is man**, that you are mindful of him, or the son of man, that you care for him? **You made him for a little while lower than the angels; you have crowned him with glory and honor, putting everything in subjection under his feet.***

Now in putting everything in subjection to him, he left nothing outside his control. At present, we do not yet see everything in subjection to him. But we see him who for a little while was made lower than the angels, namely Jesus, crowned with glory and honor because of the suffering of death, so that by the grace of God he might taste death for everyone. *Hebrews 2:6-9, ESV (emphasis mine)*

The writer of Hebrews is revealing something that had been a mystery. He starts by quoting Psalm 8. Man has been made for God's glory. While for a season we are a little lower than angels, that is not our destiny. He has put everything under our authority in this place, here on earth. We are not fully there yet, but that is His destination for His children. He left nothing here that is not under subjection to man. While we don't see that just yet, we do see Jesus, the Son of God, the Son of Man. He too was made lower than the angels for a season, so He would bring us into this great salvation we have in Christ. Now in Christ, "all things" are subject to us: illness, afflictions of body, soul, and spirit, even demons are subject to God's light bearers, His chosen vessels where He dwells. Not because of us, but because we are in Him, and He is in us; we are His Body. This is important for us to take hold of. It is this reality that allows us to destroy the works of the enemy in the power of His Spirit: Christ in us, we in Christ, we are One. We see ourselves small, but we are only temporarily lower than the angels, until we step into the fullness of sonship in Christ. This all flows from the Father's love for His Son and His Bride: the family of God.

Paul goes on to share his prayer for the Ephesians. Anytime you see an apostolic prayer, take note and make it your own.

I have not stopped giving thanks for you, remembering you in my prayers. I keep asking that the God of our Lord Jesus Christ, the glorious Father, may give you the Spirit of wisdom and revelation, so that you may know him better.
Ephesians 1:16-17

Paul is asking the Father to release the *"Spirit of wisdom and revelation"* to know who better? Jesus? No, the Father. Do not misunderstand me— Jesus is not less than the Father, as they are One. However, Jesus' mission was for us to come to the Father through Him, so we would know the Father even as He knows the Father. From here on, Paul shares the Father. It is powerful!

We are His Masterpiece

*But God, being rich in mercy, because of the great love with which he loved us, even when we were dead in our trespasses, made us alive together with Christ — by grace you have been saved — and raised us up with him and seated us with him in the heavenly places in Christ Jesus, so that in the coming ages he might show the immeasurable riches of his grace in kindness toward us in Christ Jesus. For by grace you have been saved through faith. And this is not your own doing; it is the gift of God, not a result of works, so that no one may boast. For we are His **workmanship**, created in Christ Jesus for good works, which God prepared beforehand, that we should walk in them. Ephesians 2:4-10, ESV (emphasis mine)*

Religion relegates man to strive for what has been given freely. We struggle to be worthy of the gift of grace, chasing after what has already been given. Religion always says, "You're not good enough. Work harder." Grace says, "Stop working. Rest in what I have given." It never ceases to amaze me how our natural bent is to take truth and make it religious, adding rules, steps, and disciplines to attain some perceived goodness, some illusory goal that is always just beyond our reach. In Ephesians 2, Paul starts by talking about grace by faith. Faith is not something we have to obtain. We often hear people say, "I don't think I have enough faith." I understand what they are saying because I have been there, but it is a lie. The problem is not that we don't have enough faith. The faith we need is "God's faith." We have all the faith we will ever need; we have His Spirit in us. The Holy Spirit is not diminished by our perceived lack. We appropriate faith not by attempting to stir up faith, but by resting in the truth: He is in us and desires to move through us. We are simply the vessel. He does the heavy lifting, and He has plenty of faith. Power comes through rest. When I say rest, I don't mean doing nothing. The rest I speak of comes from confidence in His love for you and knowing you and God are good.

Every part of a believer's life is to flow in grace. Grace is to flow out of our lives as well. John Wimber used to call the gifts of the Spirit "gracelets" — tokens of the love, kindness, and power of God. Faith is agreeing with God because you know and understand that power doesn't come because you are worthy, but because He is love. Salvation comes through this same spiritual mechanism, and everything else in the Kingdom does as well.

Paul shares that this grace flowed from God's great love for us. *"Because of the great love with which he loved us, even when we were dead in our trespasses, made us alive together with Christ."* We are alive *"now"* in Christ. We are presently living IN Christ. It is our perception that is clouding this reality. He goes on to say, *"… and **raised** us up with him and **seated** us with him in the heavenly places in Christ Jesus, so that in the coming ages he might show the* *immeasurable riches of his grace in kindness toward us in Christ Jesus."* We are presently raised up in Him. We are also presently seated with Him in the same way. Where? In heavenly places. Why? Because we are in Him. We are His body. We carry His authority because we are already raised up with Him in the resurrected life. The Holy Spirit is the deposit of our ownership to God, but also our position in Him. Finally, Paul moves us towards an understanding that there is something yet to be revealed *"in the coming ages."* Jesus has done so much more than simply save us from sin.

We are God's masterpiece. You are God's masterpiece. I am not making that up. It is the truth.

In the next verse, Ephesians 2:10, Paul makes this statement, *"We are his (God's)* **workmanship, created in Christ Jesus for good works,** *which* **God prepared beforehand, that we should walk in them."** The Greek word used for "workmanship" is *"poeima."* It can mean workmanship, handiwork or work of the hands, and it can also mean masterpiece. Many will argue that in the Greek Old Testament, *poeima* is used to say work, works, or deeds. Therefore, workmanship is the best definition. Most of those who would agree would do so because they focus on the sin issues Paul speaks about. However, the focus of the passage is not on their sin, but the extravagant gift of grace flowing from God's great love for us. Even if you want to stick with the word workmanship, the idea is still that the Master Creator fashioned us Himself, to do works that are good "in Christ." In Christ, we are His masterpiece. When the

Father spoke creation, we were His masterpiece. He said on the sixth day, when He made man, "It is very good." When we grasp hold of this, it should move us towards His heart. When He created all things, He declared over us, "This part of My creation is very good. They are My masterpiece." We are the one He drew close to and breathed His very breath into. Why were we declared very good? Because we are His Son's Body. We are His Son's Bride. We are His beloved children. We are His prize. We are His resting place. Take a breath, and read that again, out loud. This is who we are, not the lies, shame, fear, and insecurity tell us we are. We are His best! We are in process and yet it is finished. It is paradoxical, yet no less true.

The Mystery

> . . . *to bring to light for everyone what is the plan of the mystery hidden for ages in God, who created all things,* **so that through the church the manifold wisdom of God might now be made known to the rulers and authorities in the heavenly places.** *Ephesians 3:9-10, ESV (emphasis mine)*

For many years, I read this verse and missed out on something very significant. Eventually, it began to shift my understanding and application of the following verses. Before I share this mystery, I would like to look at the word "church" in the context of what Paul is sharing. First of all, the word church, *chirche,* is used in the Bible as we would apply it. *Chirche* is a Celt and German rendering of the Greek, *kuriakos*. This word means "the Lord's" or "belonging to a lord." It appears only twice, once referring to "The Lord's Supper," and again in Revelation referring to the "Lord's Day." In neither of those is there a reference to God's people. The word in the Greek interpreted as church is *"ekklesia."* This word means the *"gathered together ones, the called-out ones, or the assembly."* Why is this important? It will redefine our understanding and application of certain scripture. I don't mind calling the building we meet in a church, or even referring to the people who meet in that place the Church, however there is a bigger issue here. The historical background around the usage of church comes from the time Christianity became the religion of the Roman Empire. Buildings for the gods were a big deal to the people of the world. As the separation of laity and clergy took place, the assembly of the people was more and more defined by the building they met in. Buildings to gather aren't a bad thing, unless it reinterprets the original design. What I mean is simply this: When we see the building, we meet in as the measure of our service, we miss something bigger. Stay with me, please.

This word *ekklesia* means *"the called-out ones, the gathered together, or assembly."* It is applied to the governing individuals called out, elected to a life of service to help govern their community. They were brought out of the normal and mundane life to a life of service. When we apply this understanding to the scripture, the intention of the Holy Spirit is to reveal something mysterious, powerful, and definitive in identifying the followers of Jesus; namely, we have been called out of the world into a different type of civil community, a different paradigm for societal living and a different government, a community carrying a different set of values and purpose, formed out of being "in Christ, for Christ, and designed for the Father." Now, let's look at verse 10 with *ekklesia* where it should be instead of church, so *"that through the **ekklesia, those the Lord has called out from the world system, those God has assembled and gathered as His own,** the manifold* (multifaceted) *wisdom of God might now be made known to the rulers and authorities in the heavenly places."* Paul is telling us there is something in the "multifaceted" wisdom of God that can now be known to "the rulers and authorities in *heavenly places."* There is something rulers and authorities, angels of all kinds, did not know about the Father, Son, and Holy Spirit that now is being made known to them through our relationship with God, and more importantly, His relationship with us as Father. How do I know that?

> *For this reason I bow my knees before the Father, from whom every family in heaven and on earth is named, that according to the riches of his glory he may grant you to be strengthened with power through his Spirit in your inner being, so that Christ may dwell in your hearts through faith – that you, being rooted and grounded in love, may have strength to comprehend with all the saints what is the breadth and length and height and depth, and to know the love of Christ that surpasses knowledge, that you may be filled with all the fullness of God. Ephesians 3:14-19, ESV*

Paul draws our attention to two things here. First, that this is about the Father, and second, that it is about His family. We are then brought to the powerful statement, "So that Christ may dwell in our hearts through faith, that our roots would be grounded (deep and strong), our feet firmly set in *His love*." Not just some of us, but all of us together. We, all together, are to come to know how wide, long, high, and deep is His love. There is something that will make a profound adjustment in His Body—when we come together in the unity of the Spirit, the Spirit who is Love. Remember Acts 17? "In Him we live and move and have our being." This is the same Paul writing here, that we would know this love that is four dimensional. To what end? That we would be filled to ALL the *fullness of God*.

Let me wrap this up more succinctly. What we have just read is that Christ was crucified before anything was created on our behalf, so nothing was left to chance. The Father's love for you has never wavered. He was determined to have us. We are His masterpiece. Finally, His intent from the beginning was there would be something about who He is angels could not understand or perceive outside of His relationship with us, how His love causes our hearts to respond. When the Father has completely formed us in His love, there will be a revealing of something so profound, it has never been seen before. The Father's intention was and is to have offspring that carry the fullness of Him: Father, Son, and Holy Spirit. His children will choose Him because of His great love for us, transforming us into the image of His beloved Son. Holy Spirit in us, we in Christ, ALL in the Father.

Finally, through His family, He will be known in ways He was not known before. No wonder Satan wants to destroy us with fear and shame. When we step into the fullness of knowing who we are, the glory of God will cover the earth. We will truly be the light of Christ. Friends, it is all about His love. His love is nuclear. His love transforms us and will transform the world. His love is mighty to change our paradigm and position us to bring Heaven to earth in our day to day life. Counseling people, praying for healing, deliverance, restoration, reconciliation, carrying the tangible power of His love to the poor, hungry, or marginalized, simply being the hands and feet of Jesus are all expressions of love. Yes, there will be a day when darkness will rise in one final last-ditch effort to usurp what is not theirs. On that day, our King Himself will return in glory and splendor. Until then, we pursue the Father, Son, and Holy Spirit in love. We actively love those around us, making Him known. We declare the Gospel of the Kingdom. We heal the sick, cast out demons, raise the dead, feed the poor, care for widows and orphans, and care for prisoners, all in His name. We declare and demonstrate the superiority of the Kingdom of God.

Chapter 13
Shifting Your Vision

Stand therefore, having fastened on the belt of truth, and having put on the breastplate of righteousness, and, as shoes for your feet, having put on the readiness given by the gospel of peace· In all circumstances take up the shield of faith, with which you can extinguish all the flaming darts of the evil one; and take the helmet of salvation, and the sword of the Spirit, which is the word of God. Ephesians 6:14-17, ESV

When we grasp the fullness of sonship and the intention of the Father for His children, it shifts our paradigm for life. We begin to see things from Heaven's perspective and become powerful to make Him known through love, truth, and His power. If we are going to live in the fullness of what we were created for in this broken world, we need new vision, new eyes, spiritual eyes that have taken hold of the truth and can discern what is real from what is the illusion of the enemy's smoke and mirrors. This is not easily done. It is difficult to ignore what our senses tell us is real, in order for the eyes of faith to bring the superior reality of Heaven into our lives. If we are to have new eyes, we will need some new tools. Just as eyeglasses can uniquely repair our vision, we need spiritual corrective lenses to see the Kingdom reality all around us. The Scripture has given us what we need. The Holy Spirit will do the rest as we allow Him to redefine and refine some things. We need to be willing to risk and fight for the promises we have in Christ. Overcomers don't simply happen; they are born and molded through the fire. They are resolute, tenacious, and devoted to seeking Him and being completely free from everything that hinders the from moving into and living out of the depths of His love. They are powerful, counted amongst those Jesus says, *"are violent men taking heaven by force"* *Matthew 11:12.* Those who storm the gates of the Father's house declaring who He is and who they are in Him will not leave unchanged. They are like Jacob who would not let go of the Angel of the Lord without a blessing. They are those who will press through the crowd until they touch the garment of Jesus. They will not be denied the blessings they have in Christ or the calling on their life. They pursue godliness, love, humility, servanthood, integrity, honesty, kindness, purity, and goodness with the kind of perseverance and tenacity that is willing to lose everything for the blessing, even if it leaves them crippled, as it did Jacob. Are you willing to pursue your destiny as a son or daughter? I hope you are. You will never be the same again, and neither will your world.

As I said, we need a new understanding of how to take hold of all our God has for us, while standing against the enemy's schemes. There are many tools and weapons we can find in scripture. I have found "The Armor of God" in Ephesians 6 to be most helpful; however, with a bit of a different perspective than we are usually be taught.

The Armor of God and Identity

Put on the whole armor of God, that you may be able to stand against the schemes of the devil. For we do not wrestle against flesh and blood, but against the rulers, against the authorities, against the cosmic powers over this present darkness, against the spiritual forces of evil in the heavenly places. Therefore take up the whole armor of God, that you may be able to stand in the evil day, and having done all, to stand firm. Stand therefore, having fastened on **the belt of truth,** *and having* **put on the breastplate of righteousness,** *and, as* **shoes for your feet, having put on the readiness given by the gospel of peace** *In all* **circumstances take up the shield of faith,** *with which you can extinguish all the flaming darts of the evil one; and* **take the helmet of salvation, and the sword of the Spirit, which is the word of God,** *praying at all times in the Spirit, with all prayer and supplication. Ephesians 6:11-18a, ESV (emphasis mine)*

The armor of God is an important, practical revelation on how to protect yourself from the schemes and plans of the enemy. All the assaults of the enemy are generally directed at tearing down your identity and God's integrity through fear and shame. I have most often heard taught that the armor of God are symbols pointing to disciplines we must develop. For example, the breastplate of righteousness is about protecting your heart from sin, staying steadfast in doing right. Certainly, that is good, and we should be committed as best as we are able in the process, to live rightly. However, I would like to propose a slightly different perspective.

Ephesians 6:11-18 is more than a statement regarding practice or disciplines. It speaks more decisively about the importance of identity, if we are to stand against the schemes and plans of the evil one. The battle we fight is against the cosmic powers of darkness, the spiritual forces in heavenly places. In chapter 6, we looked at 1 Corinthians 10:3-5. This scripture sheds some light here as well. *"The weapons we fight with are not the weapons of the world. On the contrary, they have divine power to demolish strongholds. We demolish arguments and every pretension that sets itself up against the knowledge of God."* Our weapons of defense and offense are focused on standing against the lies that come between God and His children. There are two key areas the enemy attacks the believer. One is the goodness, love, and character of God, His trustworthiness. The other is our place in His family, our sonship. In the Garden, the serpent engaged Eve with a conversation implying the integrity, honesty, and trustworthiness of our Father was questionable. In doing so, he stole our identity, calling, and intimacy with God. In the wilderness, the enemy tempted Jesus in the same two areas. The first temptation concerned the Father's heart and Jesus knowing His Father's faithfulness to sustain Him. *"If you are the son of God turn these stones to bread."*

The next was, *"If you are the Son, throw yourself down and prove it."* This is the second assault against His identity and His Father's integrity. The "if you are" tactic comes in different forms, but it is always intended to tear down the walls of relational strength, authority, and power that are rooted in knowing who you are and who God is to you. The enemy always is working to separate you from your Heavenly Father.

The third is, *"He said to him, 'All these I will give you, if you will fall down and worship me.'"* Satan wants us to take the promises of God into our own hands, without the surrender to His will necessary to form us to maturity in His image. In the wilderness, Satan offered Jesus what the Father already determined to accomplish, but without the cost. That is exactly the same trap he led Adam and Eve into in the Garden. Eat it, and you will get there more quickly. It looks good for the gaining of wisdom. You won't have to wait. You can have it now. The problem is, the goal of the Father is that we would be His tabernacle and that we would love exactly like He does. It is in His love where true wisdom lives.

If we are to correctly understand and apply "The Armor of God," we must look at it in this context, standing against and protecting ourselves from these lies that lead to ruin, and the arguments that exalt themselves and stand in the way of knowing the Lord intimately.

The Belt of Truth

First, the belt of truth. The word "truth" in the Greek is *"alithiea."* It is a noun and has a fascinating meaning. It is the same word used in John 14:16, when Jesus says, *"I am the way, the truth, and the life."* It means "unconcealedness, the revealing of the hidden things." It also means reality. In the Gospel of John, Jesus is saying He is to define our reality. Our paradigm, our world view, is to be founded in Him—who He is and His ways. Here, Paul is telling the Ephesians to protect their weakest places with the reality of who they are in Christ and who their Father is. We are to hold to the reality we are His sons and daughters, His family, His possession. Don't listen to lies thrown at you to contradict this truth.

The Breastplate of Righteousness

The Greek word used here for "righteousness" is *"dikaiosune."* It means, "to be in the right, to have the judge's approval, to be *'approved by God.'"* Paul is telling us to let our heart rest because we are at peace with the Father by the blood of Jesus. Don't let your emotions go anywhere but to rest in your right relationship in Christ with your Heavenly Father. We can rest in this reality because Jesus says so. It is His blood that cleanses us. While we may struggle with sin, we are not sinners; we are sons and daughters made righteous by the shed blood. When your emotions rise up to say otherwise, remember who you are.

Feet Fitted with the Gospel of Peace

I used to think this phrase meant I should always be ready to share the Gospel. Certainly we should be, and there is power in doing so. However, I now believe there is something else to discern here. Paul is getting revelation while observing a Roman soldier guarding him. He notices something about his sandals, the sandals of a warrior. They have spikes in them to keep the soldier from losing their footing in the midst of battle. Their feet are firmly set on the ground beneath them. I like the way Kris Vallotton shares this. He says let your understanding, your foundation, the thing that cannot be shaken, be in the Gospel of Peace. What is the Gospel of Peace? God the Father and God the Son are at peace with us, the proof being His very Spirit we carry within us. This readiness that comes from being fitted with the Gospel of Peace means we can stand and share with confidence that through Jesus, His death and resurrection, man can be in perfect peace with God. Once you receive Christ as Lord and Savior, there is only peace between you and the Maker of Heaven and earth. No more fear, shame, or doubt, only peace exists between you and Him. "But I still sin," you say. Yes, you are in process. Jesus didn't die only for your sins before you came to Him. He died for ALL sin - past, present, and future. All of it is covered by the Blood. Simply repent, turn towards Him, surrender to Him, and move on. Don't allow yourself to stand on sinking sand. Trust in Him and be at peace. Then you will be able to fully share the Good News with others, because you understand His great love.

The Shield of Faith

This is a simple one to unwrap. First, note that like the sword, this is not attached to your body. You must hold it in your hand. The fiery darts come from many directions. What are these fiery darts? The lies of the enemy that come into our thoughts and the accusations we hold against others. What is faith? It is agreeing wholeheartedly with something that cannot be seen. Fear is faith in what we don't want. It is agreement. How do we use this shield of faith? We don't agree with the lies, and instead, we grasp hold of the truth of Father God, reflected in Jesus. We stand on the reality of who He is, who we are in Him, and all that He says is true. Whenever anything comes against right relationship with the Lord, we say no, and apply what we know is right and true in Jesus. We agree only with what His word says, especially regarding the two schemes of the enemy — who we are and who God is to us. When the assault comes, you say no to the lie and take hold of what has been promised.

The Helmet of Salvation

Salvation, "sótéria" in the Greek, is a powerful word when we understand the full extent of its meaning. Generally, when we hear the word salvation, our application is limited. We were going towards destruction, and Jesus saved us. He extended an invitation for salvation. This is certainly a good and right application, and I am thankful for this meaning. However, like so many other words we have already discussed, salvation is much more than having been saved from Hell. This word sótéria means deliverance from all our enemies in every area of life. It means preservation in our physical life. It means provision for our natural life. It offers peace for our soul. This great salvation gives us everything that was lost in the Garden: intimacy with our Father, resting in His peace, protection from our enemies, confidence in His provision and protection, and the guarantee of our purposes in Him. If the enemy can't get to your heart, he will go for your head, and vice versa. Just as we guard our hearts with the reality we are right with God, we must guard our thought life, holding to the truth the Cross covers every need we have physically, emotionally, and spiritually. Remember, the enemy attacks who you are as a child of God and who God is as your Father. One way he does this is by slipping thoughts into our mind that may seem like our own, but are not. These thoughts attack His goodness and kindness, as we have discussed earlier. They attack His trustworthiness to protect, provide, and guide you into the fullness of all He has for you. When Paul speaks of the helmet of salvation, he is telling us to make no room for thoughts that war against all the Cross has accomplished for us. Jesus paid the price in every area of life. Your family may have suffered from lack, but His blood broke that off of you, and you now have a good Father who is a good provider. Broken relationships may have followed you your whole life, but His blood covers all of that, and you now have the Spirit of Love in you to guide you. There may be terrible failure in your family line, but the blood of Jesus breaks the power of everything present in your natural family line. By His blood, you are now part of an eternal family whose Father covers everything lost in the Garden. When those thoughts pop up, recognize they are lies, and remember the Cross took care of it all. You and your Heavenly Father are in perfect peace together, that old lying identity has no right to taunt you any longer. Don't agree with those lying thoughts. Declare and prophesy over yourself all that is promised. He will provide for you and yours through His perfect sacrifice.

The Sword of the Spirit, which is the Word of God

"The sword which is the Word," — what an amazing statement. It is the only offensive weapon we have been given, and it is all we need. It is powerful.

The Father is working out His intention, His aim and desire for His children. He is doing it with fiery passion. He will not be dissuaded or distracted. He is resolute. He will have His heart's desire. Nothing can stop it from coming to fruition. He has all the bases covered. We need not fear. There are two words in the Greek for "word," one is *logos* and the other is *rhema*. The word *Logos* is applied to the pre-incarnate Christ, the second Person of the Trinity. He is the perfect communication and revelation of the Godhead. He is the eternal Word. *Logos* is also used to reference the entirety of His written word, the scripture. Hebrews 4:12 says, "*For the word of God is alive and active. Sharper than any double-edged sword, it penetrates even to dividing soul and spirit, joints and marrow; it judges the thoughts and attitudes of the heart.*" The writer of Hebrews is declaring that the full Word of God, inspired by the Holy Spirit, is alive and working, revealing His truth and His reality. This is a good and true word.

In Ephesians 6:17, we read *"the sword of the Spirit, which is the word of God."* Here, "word" is *rhema*. It is important to understand the difference. While a certain scripture can be a rhema word, it is only a rhema word when the Spirit leads you to it. If the Spirit breathes life on a specific verse or verses, it is a rhema word, a word in the moment. It is a God-breathed word for the moment, situation, or season. However, it isn't limited to only scripture. It can be a prophetic word given for the specific purpose, to bring light to what God is doing now or will be doing in the future. When the sword is a rhema word, you can expect to get the word from two or three, so you will have confidence it is the Lord.

> *"Man shall not live by bread alone, but by every word [**rhema**] that proceeds out of the mouth of God." Matthew 4:4, NASB (emphasis mine)*

> *"The words [**rhema**] that I speak to you are spirit, and they are life." John 6:63, NKJV (emphasis mine)*

A rhema word is a word that will have life and power on it on your behalf. These prophetic words are powerful against the schemes of the enemy. As he assaults with lies, we can declare with faith, both the scripture and prophecies we have been given, with confidence, authority, and expectation that our Father will move on our behalf.

Wrapping Up the Armor of God

I hope you can see the armor of God in this light and understand how to stand against the enemy. Stand firm in your sonship, in His goodness, kindness, grace, and love. Hold on to hope. Agree with what He has promised you, both as part of His family, and in the personal words He has given you. One of my favorite scriptures is Ephesians 1:18-20. *"I pray that the eyes of your heart may be enlightened in order that you may know the hope to which he has called you, the riches of his glorious inheritance in his holy people, and his incomparably great power for us who believe. That power is the same as the mighty strength he exerted when he raised Christ from the dead and seated him at his right hand in the heavenly realms."* In a season of transition, when I was battling to hold on to my identity, the Spirit spoke these words into me to make them my prophetic prayer and declaration. He took a *logos* word and made it a *rhema* word, God-breathed for the moment. In this season, he also had others give me prophetic words that lined up with scripture. I could take *rhema* words, scripture, and prophecy, and use them as my sword. I was fighting off lies that were coming against my identity and His great love for me.

Stand firm in who you are. Stand firm in His great love. Stand firm that you and your Heavenly Father are at peace because of Jesus and His finished work on the Cross. Stand firm that nothing can separate you from His love, not even your own thoughts and emotions. Put on the full armor and remember who you are.

Wrapping it Up

God is forming us to be like Him in the fullness of Christ. We are in process. He is forming us into the people of His intentions. We are the temple of God — the hands, feet, and heart of God made known in the most unique way: relationally, a Father and His children.

This forming is done in two layers: the working into us His heart and mind and His will and purpose, and the working out of His ways and revealed love. The second layer causes us to reflect Him so accurately. We shine forth, releasing His presence and causing spiritual atmospheres to shift and line up with Heaven, making Him known as He truly is, not as a religious or manmade replica. We are a prophetic people. What does that mean? Everything the Lord does comes with a speaking forth that releases the Spirit to move according to the Father's will. In the beginning, God spoke, the Spirit moved, and creation came forth. The Holy Spirit desires to move similarly in us, His children. This is one reason James talks about the power of the tongue to release blessing or cursing. Our words have power. When we think of prophecy, we most often think of foretelling prophecy — the revealing of a future event. That is only one expression of the Spirit moving in prophecy. There is also "forth-telling" prophecy. Forth-telling prophecy functions through the spoken word inspired by the Holy Spirit. This type of prophecy causes situations to shift and line up with God's will. When Jesus rebuked the storm, it was a type of forth-telling. It looks a lot like the creation story: "Let there be light," and there was light. Our words have power, and they impact atmospheres in more ways than we realize. As His children, we have a prophetic calling to declare the truth of the Kingdom. If we could understand who we are in Christ and what He has called us to, we would see so many things shift around us. Satan doesn't want us to take hold of who we are. If we did, his kingdom would be ransacked. When we see Jesus speak healing, it is a prophetic utterance of forth-telling. He is speaking into a condition, declaring in faith the Kingdom reality, forth-telling wholeness, and it becomes so.

So, what are we missing? Many of us don't fully believe or understand we are sons and daughters, carrying the very presence of the living God within us. All too often, our religious attitudes and brokenness causes us to misunderstand the heart and mind of God. We so often miss the heart of the Father, and it causes us to pursue ministry in ways that are not His heart. We have not because we ask not, and when we do ask, we are lacking faith or have wrong motives. When our hearts and minds line up and are fully surrendered to the Lord, we will know what to ask for, and we will see those requests fulfilled. Again, God is IN you. The Father doesn't simply want a job done. He wants all creation to rejoice in who He is. He is Love. His love given and expressed towards us is exactly the way He loves all creation. We were birthed from Him, from love, and this love between us is making Him known, transforming our lives and the lives of those around us, bringing Heaven to earth.

The Father's intention is to have a family that loves Him, loves each other, makes Him known and rules and reigns at His side in such a way that all creation will see Him in new ways. I love family. I love sharing life with family and friends. I love that ultimately, our Heavenly Father feels the same way. Isn't that great news!

I pray you go deeper and deeper in His love daily. That you come to a place of such deep understanding and experience of Him, that all fear is shattered, and you live the powerful, overcoming, world-changing life you were made for. God is so very good and kind. He loves you with an undying, mountain moving, overcoming, atomically powerful love. You can say He loves you with ALL that He is. Darkness can't comprehend it. All those who are His will come to rest in Him. May you rest in His love! Bless you!

Section Six

The Parable of the Great Eagle

and the Vulture

The Parable of the Great Eagle and the Vulture

Dedicated to my grandson, Judah, and all my future grandchildren.

"Daddy," little Judah said, "the boys down the block were calling me mean names. Telling me I wasn't good enough to play ball with them."

"Boys can sometimes be mean," his dad told him. "You will run into people in life that say things that hurt you. People that are hurting inside say hurtful things. Don't ever let them tell you who you are. There is only one opinion that matters, Jesus'. He loves you perfectly."

Judah look puzzled and asked, "Why do people say mean things to people?"

"Well Judah, that is not as simple a question as you may think. Come sit with me. I want to tell you a story."

There once was a Great Eagle and a Vulture who soared over the same mountain range and valley. The Great Eagle made his home in a crevice near the highest point on the highest mountain. Nestled between rocks and crags, he and his mate built a strong nest, safe from the elements and perfectly suited for their soon to be family. The Vulture, on the other hand, lived in the dry, hot, windless valley. He made his home on the branch of an almost dead tree, surrounded by mostly dead and dry brambles. All around were the bones of the dead carcasses he fed on.

The Vulture hated the Great Eagle passionately. He hated his beauty and majesty. He hated the high place where he lived. He hated that the Great Eagle was revered and honored. He wanted to be like the Great Eagle, but knew he was nothing like him, and he hated him all the more for it. In fact, he wanted the Great Eagle dead, but knew he was not capable of killing him. One day, while flying high, the Vulture noticed the Great Eagle's nest in the midst of the rocks on top of the highest mountain. He thought to himself, "Great, that eagle is going to have offspring, and this place is going to be even more filled with eagles. I hate him, I hate them." Then a devious, despicable, evil thought came to his mind. He thought, "I will wait for the eggs to be laid in the nest, and when the eagles are away, flying around, I will sneak in and take as many eggs as I can. I will raise them to believe they are vultures. That will teach him. I will break his heart."

And so the evil Vulture did just that. He snuck up there and stole three eggs. He brought them down into that dry, dead valley. He sat on them until they hatched, and when they did, he executed his plan. He never allowed them to see him fly, and he told them, "You are my offspring. You are vultures. Vultures can't fly. Vultures live in this dry valley amongst dead carcasses. They eat dead, rotten meat, and they die right here in this valley." Over time, the young eagles believed the Vulture was their father and that they were vultures, even though they realized they didn't quite look like him. Why would their father lie to them? So, they lived in the dry, dead valley, never taking flight, and living on dead, rotting meat, which they found very unsatisfying and quite disgusting. They spent their days and nights walking in the valley, never flying, and feeling alone.

One day, the Great Eagle was flying over the valley, and with his keen sight, he noticed three fairly young eagles walking around in the dry, lifeless valley. He couldn't help but notice that by their size, they were long past the age of flight. Out of curiosity, he flew down to speak with them, to see why they were so skinny, unhealthy, and not flying.

He swooped down and landed in front of them with a great wind caused by his immense wing span. He majestically stood in front of the deceived young eagles. He asked, "What are you young ones doing down here? You are well past the age of flight. You should be up in the sky soaring at great heights."

They were stunned at this stranger, and his words scared them. As if rehearsed, they replied, "Oh no, no, no. We are vultures, and vultures can't fly. Please go. If our father sees us speaking to you, he will be very angry and will punish us terribly."

The Great Eagle asked, "Who told you are vultures?"

"Our father, the great Vulture," they said.

"You are not vultures. You are Great Eagles, like me. You were created to fly amongst the highest clouds, over the highest mountains, across great oceans of green grass, over great distances."

The young eagles didn't want to listen. This would surely catch them a beating when their father came home. "Please go," they said.

The Great Eagle said, "Let me ask you one more question. May I do that?"

"Well, okay," they said. "But then you must go."

"Whom do you look more like, your so-called father, or me? In whose likeness were you born?"

They looked at each other, back and forth a few times, and then at him, stunned by the question and how much they looked like him. One said timidly, "Well, we kind of look like you."

"Kind of? You are the spitting image of me. You are eagles. You were made for greatness, the most majestic creatures in the air. You were not made to walk in the dust. You were made to soar amongst the clouds."

The young eagles didn't know what to say. They just stood there in complete silence. Then, the Great Eagle said something they were completely unprepared for. "A long time ago, my mate and I had three eggs; they were going to be our first offspring. We were joyful with expectation. One day, while we were busy preparing for their arrival, our eggs were taken from the nest. We frantically searched everywhere for them, but could not find them. You are our lost children. Come; let me teach you how to fly. I will show you the beauty and majesty that is all around you, outside of this dead valley."

"Oh no, no, no," one spoke.

Another said, "We can't fly. We are vultures. Our father wouldn't lie to us, would he?"

The third young eagle said, "I would like to try. I have always felt like there was more for us than this place."

The Great Eagle stepped towards them with his wings fully open. The sheer size of his wing span was enough to block the sun from the young eagles. The Great Eagle said, "Spread out your wings, all the way like mine."

The first young eagle said, "I will not. I cannot fly. I am not an eagle. I am a vulture who is stuck to the ground. My father says so. He surely would not lie to me." And with a huff, he began to walk away, commanding his brothers, "Don't listen to this trouble maker. If you do, father is going to punish you hard. Come with me now."

However, the other two wanted to try. One, because he was curious, the other, because he wanted more than the life he had. Something in him believed the Great Eagle. They both spread their wings wide. The Great Eagle started running and flapping his great wings in a smooth, full rhythm. As he did, he began to lift off the ground, and ever so gracefully, went higher and higher above the valley. He majestically circled round, went into a dive, pulled up, suddenly opening his wings, and came to a soft, graceful landing in front of the young ones.

"Now you do exactly like I did," He said. "Open your wings, run, and flap smoothly in rhythm — one… two… one… two. As you come up off the ground, make the spreading and contracting of your wings more open and less close. When you get high enough, your instincts will kick in, and you will catch the wind and soar."

The curious one went first. He started to run, flapping his wings frantically, lifted off the ground, and immediately fell on his face. Again, he tried, and his believing brother with him. As they ran and flapped, they lifted just slightly off the ground, but fell again. Once more they tried, and again, they fell. The curious young eagle said to the Great Eagle, "I told you. We are not like you. We may look like you, but we are obviously vultures. We can't fly. We just flop to the ground. Why do you taunt us and tease us this way? I can't fly. None of us can. Take your lies and leave us alone, before our father returns and punishes us."

However, the third young eagle, the one who said he believed in something more, had a different perception of what happened. He said, "Brother, didn't you feel it?"

His brother answered, "Feel what? I felt nothing but my body hitting the ground and my beak full of dirt."

The unbelieving brother, standing a short distance away on a dead branch, was laughing. "You two looked ridiculous. It was funny watching you fall face first. Do it again. I want to laugh more at your foolishness."

The curious brother turned and said, "Shut up. At least I was willing to try. Now I know it is true. We are vultures."

The other yelled back, "Well, I knew that and didn't have to make a fool of myself to figure it out." He laughed again, with a deep belly laugh. The curious brother looked at him from the corner of his eye, wanting to say something, but knowing if he did, he would just be made fun of again. After all, he did look foolish.

Now, the brother who believed looked at them both and smiled. He said, "You didn't see what I saw. You didn't experience what I experienced because you didn't want to. You missed out on the wonderful part of what just happened."

They looked at him confused. What did they miss? They yelled to him, "What did we miss, you fool? You flapped your wings and fell face first."

He said, "Yes I did, but for one moment, my feet were completely off the ground, and I could feel flight."

Right then, the Great Eagle spoke, "That's it, son. You experienced the miracle, just a little, and held on to it. You now know the truth. It is possible to fly. It is in you. You just need to keep pressing forward."

The young, believing eagle said, "Yes, yes, yes. I want to feel that again!"

The Great Eagle said, "Come with me, and let's do it together." The Great Eagle took him up on a long ledge about eight feet above the valley and said, "Let's run together here. You follow me, doing exactly as I do. I have taken you a little higher. It seems riskier, and it is, but you will fly higher now than before."

The Great Eagle ran, opening and closing his wings, and just as he was about to reach the end, he came up off the ground, wings open, dipped, flapped one great flap, and took off. "Now you do exactly as I did," he yelled back to the young eagle.

His brothers were screaming at him, "Don't do it. You are going to break your neck!"

He looked at them and smiled, while under his breath he said, "I am not going to break my neck. I am going to fly. I am a great majestic eagle."

With that, he ran, mimicking exactly what his teacher, his true father, showed him. As he reached the end of the path, he came off the ground just slightly and dipped down. He didn't let fear grab hold of him. He knew he was a great eagle. Instead, he opened and closed his wings more rapidly. He lifted his head up, and just before he hit the ground, he took off upward, going higher and higher. In no time, his two brothers were small figures below him. As he caught the wind, he made a wide turn, looking down at the valley where he lived for so long. It all seemed so much smaller from up here. He thought about how big it always seemed to him and how overwhelming it was. Now it was so small as he gazed upon the vast mountains, forests, and green fields outside the valley he knew as home. He took another wide circle around the mountain and went back to the valley.

"Brothers, it is true. It is all true. We are eagles. We can fly. We can soar even above the mountains. There is so much more for us than we have been able to see."

The first brother, the unbelieving one, said, "I don't believe you. It is a trick, and even if you could fly, I know I cannot. Our father has told us so. I know there is no greatness in me. Leave me alone. I don't want to hear your foolish tales. Everyone knows vultures can't fly."

He couldn't see or understand what his brother was telling him. He couldn't believe he was foolish enough to believe a lie his whole life. As he walked away, he muttered to himself under his breath, "This can't be true. If it is, my whole life has been a lie. I can't accept that. It would mean everything I have been taught is wrong, a flat out lie. That would make me the biggest fool of all. No, no, no... it simply cannot be true."

With that, he looked back over his shoulder and gave a parting word to his believing brother, "When you break your neck trying to be something you are not, don't expect me to pick you up, you fool."

The other brother, the one who was curious but quit, looked at his brother and saw the Great Eagle in him. He asked, "Is it really true? All that you said — the green fields, the mountains, and forests, the lakes and rivers teeming with fish — is it all true?"

"Yes, it is," he answered. "Come with me. Let me show you."

The curious brother looked at him sadly, saying, "But I failed before. I fell right on my face, and I didn't have enough faith to risk like you, my brother." It was hard for him to imagine the bird in front of him was actually the brother he once knew. His brother looked more and more like the Great Eagle.

The brave brother said, "Brother, remember? I fell too, just like you. You can quit now, or you can trust me and the Great Eagle, and risk with me. If you don't, you will never know and experience what I have seen. If you keep trying, I will be right here, and together, we will watch you soar. Learning something new takes time. It is a process. But I am the proof for you. We are brothers; there is nothing I can do that you can't. Just trust and believe."

The curious one eagerly said, "I will. I am going to keep going until I fly."

His brother replied, "I will be right here, helping you and cheering you on."

And so the curious one tried, and the other helped, and it didn't take too long for the two brothers to soar high together with the Great Eagle. Every now and then, they go back to their unbelieving brother. The Great Eagle goes with them because he loves all his children. They sit with their lost brother in the valley and encourage him in who he really was. His shame-filled belief that he was something less, and his fear of his evil, lying stepfather the Vulture kept him from trying. He stayed lost, alone, and sad in the valley. This broke the brothers' hearts, but the Great Eagle always said to them, "You don't understand everything. Don't be afraid. I will not give up on him and neither should you. There is still time. Just believe. For now, come fly with me."

The two brothers lifted off the ground together and yelled back over their shoulders to their unbelieving brother in the valley, "We aren't giving up on you. You will be with us someday."

Somehow, the brother left behind was comforted by that. He wondered, "Even after all these years, is it still possible for me? Maybe it is?"

"Daddy," young Judah asked, "what is the meaning of this story?"

His dad replied, "Judah, there are many things in this world that want you to believe you are less than you are. We have an enemy, Satan, the devil, and he is always working against people, to keep them captive to his lies and hold them back from their true destiny – the very reason the Lord made them. Just like the eagle that believed he was a vulture, many people, because of shame, are unwilling to believe God loves them and made them for something wonderful. To know God and to fly with Him, you must first believe you truly are His child, especially when people (or your own thoughts) say you are not. Judah, when you struggle to believe, remember God is right there with you, just like the Great Eagle was there to help them learn to fly and come alongside them no matter how long it took. Jesus is always right there with you. His Holy Spirit guides you. He said He will never ever leave you. The Great Eagle was there because he knew they were his sons, even though they didn't know it themselves. Once he found them, he wasn't going to leave them there in that dead valley, not even the last one that seemed hopeless. As long as there was breath in that hopeless son, the Great Eagle was going to pursue him. God will never leave us in our dark places either. He will always come for us. Likewise, we should never stop loving and hoping for those that don't know Him. We don't know or understand all the Father is doing around us. We can only follow Him and love well."

"Thanks, Dad. I understand."

"Good. Judah, I love you. More than the stars."

"I love you too, Dad. I love you to infinity and back again a hundred million times."

"I know you do, Buddy. And me, you."

"Let's play. Throw me a high one, Daddy!"

"Okay, make sure you get your glove up."

"I will."

Other Books by Coaching Saints

RECKLESS MERCY: A TROPHY OF GOD'S GRACE
BY CARL TUTTLE

Carl Tuttle has been a recipient of God's lavish love. In *Reckless Mercy,* Carl shares his story of experiencing God's ceaseless mercies through his journey of international acclaim, public downfall, and eventual restoration. As an integral leader in the birthing of the Vineyard Movement, Carl shares unique insights into the movement as well as its founder, John Wimber, a personal mentor and dear friend to Carl. In his characteristically disarming style, Carl shares the heartaches and humors of his story and takes the reader on a journey of exploring the unending and reckless mercies of God.

FROM THE SANCTUARY TO THE STREETS: INSIGHTS AND ADVENTURES IN POWER EVANGELISM
BY CHARLES BELLO AND BRIAN BLOUNT

From the Sanctuary to the Streets is a practical guide written to propel the reader into a lifestyle marked by intimacy with God and power evangelism. Through teaching and personal stories, the authors share with humor and honesty their own efforts to embrace the empowering activity of the Holy Spirit. As the authors state, "We are not called to be spiritual recluses or trail blazing burnouts. Rather, we are called to be friends of God who live a life of intimacy and impact as we simply do life with God in a naturally supernatural way."

PRAYER AS A PLACE: SPIRITUALITY THAT TRANSFORMS
BY CHARLES BELLO

Prayer as a Place is an invitation to partner with Christ as he leads the believer into the dark places of his or her own heart. The purpose of this journey is to bring holiness and wholeness to the child of God. With candor and brutal honesty, Pastor Charles Bello shares his own reluctance and then resolve to follow Christ on this inward journey. In sharing his story, readers gain insight into what their own personal journeys may look like. *Prayer as a Place* reads like a road map as it explores the contemporary use of contemplative prayer as a means of following Christ inward.

RECYCLED SPIRITUALITY: ANCIENT WAYS MADE NEW
BY CHARLES BELLO

Recycled *Spirituality* is like browsing through a mysterious, ancient resale shop filled with treasures from the rich heritage of historical Christianity. Many of the ancient spiritual disciplines have continued to be in use for thousands of years — others are being newly rediscovered. These classical disciplines are drawn from our shared Catholic, Orthodox, Protestant, Evangelical and Pentecostal traditions. The purpose of these disciplines is always transformation, renewal and missional living. As Charles writes, "The gift of tradition is meant to be received. The essence of tradition is meant to be rediscovered. And if the practice of a tradition helps form you into the image of Christ, it is meant to be recycled."

FOR MORE TITLES, VISIT:
WWW.COACHINGSAINTS.COM

CPSIA information can be obtained
at www.ICGtesting.com
Printed in the USA
BVHW032309101022
649105BV00006B/18